P9-DVC-211

DATE DUE

WILLIAM CARLOS WILLIAMS

Modern Critical Views

These and other titles in preparation

Modern Critical Views

WILLIAM CARLOS WILLIAMS

Edited and with an introduction by
Harold Bloom
Sterling Professor of the Humanities
Yale University

CHELSEA HOUSE PUBLISHERS ◊ 1986
New York ◊ New Haven ◊ Philadelphia

© 1986 by Chelsea House Publishers, a division of Chelsea House
Educational Communications, Inc.
   133 Christopher Street, New York, NY 10014
   345 Whitney Avenue, New Haven, CT 06511
   5014 West Chester Pike, Edgemont, PA 19028

Introduction © 1986 by Harold Bloom

Printed and bound in the United States of America

∞ The paper used in this publication meets the minimum
requirements of the American National Standard for Permanence of
Paper for Printed Library Materials, Z39.48–1984.

Library of Congress Cataloging-in-Publication Data
William Carlos Williams.
   (Modern critical views)
   Bibliography: p.
   Includes index.
   Summary: A collection of critical essays on Williams
and his works. Also includes a chronology of events in
his life.
   1. Williams, William Carlos, 1883–1963—Criticism
and interpretation.   [1. Williams, William Carlos,
1883–1963—Criticism and interpretation.   2. American
literature—History and criticism]   I. Bloom, Harold.
II. Series.
PS3545.I544Z9567   1986   811'.52   86-8307
ISBN 0-87754-637-1 (alk. paper)

Contents

Editor's Note

This book gathers together a representative selection of the best criticism so far devoted to the achievement of William Carlos Williams, arranged in the chronological order of its original publication. I am grateful to Susan Lasher for her assistance in editing this volume.

The editor's introduction centers upon the experimental writings now gathered together under the title *Imaginations* and on the extraordinary shorter poem, "A Unison." Louis L. Martz, the distinguished critic of the meditative mode in Anglo-American poetry, begins the chronological sequence with his now classic essay on Williams's "personal epic," *Paterson*. Martz elegantly contextualizes the long poem in much of Williams's crucial work, including *In the American Grain*, and several of the earlier shorter poems.

J. Hillis Miller follows with his generous and influential estimate of Williams as a post-metaphysical "poet of reality," indeed as someone who actually broke through into an original sense of immanence. In an equally enthusiastic overview of Williams's rather curious prose fictions, Thomas R. Whitaker also emphasizes the writer's quest for a new spirituality. Another passionately committed exegete, Joseph N. Riddel, working in the interpretive mode of Jacques Derrida, proceeds to read Williams's poetry as a grand instance of post-Heideggerian sensibility at work, presumably demonstrating that language creates man.

Riddel's ecstatic celebration is complemented by Paul Mariani's immensely informed rethinking of *Paterson*, a revisionary account not less admiring than Mariani's major biography of Williams. The poet Donald Hall wryly notes how deftly Williams invented a new kind of *visual* arrangement for a poem, in a very American gesture, a gesture studied in its larger forms in John W. Erwin's examination of Williams's stance toward Europe. Finally, Stephen Cushman sympathetically but firmly demonstrates that Williams's celebrated new "measure" is itself a trope, or troping of form, rather than the breakthrough into immanence celebrated by Williams's characteristic polemics. Cushman thus, in some ways, returns this book to its introduction, where the limits of Williams's art receive some modest consideration.

Introduction

In his critical biography *William Carlos Williams: A New World Naked*, Paul Mariani wisely asserts the lasting influence of John Keats's poetry upon even the late phases of Williams:

> The voice he *was* listening to, and the voice that struck paydirt for him, was a matter of a complex crossing with Keats, especially the Keats of the *Hyperion* fragments and the odes. Why this should have been so is difficult to say with any exactness, for Williams himself probably did not understand why. What *he* thought he was "capturing" was the voice of the classics—the stately rhythms and sharp straightforward idiom of the Greeks as he thought they must sound should they be discovered walking the streets of his Paterson. But there was something more, a kinship Williams had felt with Keats for over half a century, the plight of the romantic poet who would have spoken as the gods speak if only he had had the power to render their speech in the accents of his own debased language. *Hyperion* is in part the portrait of the dying of the ephebe into the life of the major poet, and Keats had aborted it at the very moment that his poet was undergoing that transformation.
>
> And so with Williams, opting for the step-down line as his "classic" signature as he surfaced from the realization of his mortality, the new rhythm providing a stately, slow saraband to echo Keats's Miltonic and Dantesque phase with a difference. The crossing with Keats is there too in the nature of Williams's late iconography, in the stasis of his late images, frozen for eternity in the realized artifact, as in Williams's translation from Theocritus's first idyl, with its images limned on a "two-eared bowl / of ivy-wood," a girl and two young

men, an ancient fisherman, and a small boy preoccupied with "plait-
ing a pretty / cage of locust stalks and asphodel." The images of
Asphodel too belong to the same strain: sharply realized but without
Williams's earlier breathlessness and jagged line cuttings.

Poetic influence, an intensely problematical process, normally brings together a strong poet's earliest and final phases. Williams's true precursor, necessarily composite and in some sense imaginary, was a figure that fused Keats with
Walt Whitman. Such a figure has in it the potential for a serious splitting of the
poetic ego in its defense against the poetic past. The "negative capability" of
Keats sorts oddly with Whitman's rather positive capability for conveying the
powerful press of himself. "Memory is a kind / of accomplishment," Williams
wrote in "The Descent," a crucial poem in his *The Desert Music* (1954). The
descent to dying beckons to a return of the dead precursors in one's own colors,
even as Keats and Whitman beckoned Williams to ascend into his own poetry.
But the poem "The Descent" Williams shrewdly quarried from Book 2 of his
own major long poem, *Paterson*, a quarrying that suggests his pride in his own
continuities.

Those continuities are massive throughout Williams's best work, which
can be cataloged (against the numerous Williams idolators) as a limited yet still
remarkably diverse canon: *Paterson* (Book I), *Kora in Hell*, *Spring and All*, "The
Widow's Lament in Springtime," "To Waken an Old Lady," "The Trees," "The
Yachts," "A Coronal," "These," "The Poor," "A Marriage Ritual," "Raleigh
Was Right," "Burning the Christmas Greens," "A Unison," and the grand return
of Keats-as-Williams in *Asphodel, That Greeny Flower*. Every critic I have chosen
for this volume would select more, much more, but I am of the school of Wallace Stevens, rather than of Williams, and the Williams I honor is the author of
about a dozen shorter poems, and four remarkable long poems and prose or
verse sequences. I write this introduction not to dissent, but as an experiment. If
you believe—as I do—that Williams is not of the eminence of Stevens and
Robert Frost, of Hart Crane and even of T. S. Eliot, then what is the irreducible
achievement that survives even an extreme skepticism as to Williams's poetic
greatness?

Of the volumes that collect Williams, I return most often to *Imaginations*,
edited by Webster Schott (1979), which gathers together four weird American
originals—*Kora in Hell*, *Spring and All*, *The Great American Novel*, *The Descent of Winter*—as well as some miscellaneous prose. *Kora in Hell* was subtitled
Improvisations by Williams, who had a particular fondness for it. He analogized
its astonishing "Prologue" to *On the Sublime* by the pseudo-Longinus, a comparison not so farfetched as he himself asserted it to be. Essentially it, and all of

Kora, is a collection of what Emerson (following Plutarch and Cudworth) called "lustres" (Ezra Pound's *lustra*), aphoristic impressions drawn either from others or from the self. Its center is in Williams's characteristic polemic against Pound and Eliot, with an ironizing boost from Stevens:

> E. P. is the best enemy United States verse has. He is interested, passionately interested—even if he doesn't know what he is talking about. But of course he does know what he is talking about. He does not, however, know everything, not by more than half. The accordances of which Americans have the parts and the colors but not the completions before them pass beyond the attempts of his thought. It is a middle-aging blight of the imagination.
>
> I praise those who have the wit and courage, and the conventionality, to go direct toward their vision of perfection in an objective world where the signposts are clearly marked, viz., to London. But confine them in hell for their paretic assumption that there is no alternative but their own groove.
>
> Dear fat Stevens, thawing out so beautifully at forty! I was one day irately damning those who run to London when Stevens caught me up with his mild: "But where in the world will you have them run to?"

The shrewd link to *On the Sublime* is that Williams (admirably and accurately) shares the conviction of Longinus that the Sublime or strong poetry either is agonistic or it is nothing. Williams too seeks to persuade the reader to forsake easier pleasures (Eliot and Pound) for more difficult pleasures (*Kora in Hell*). And his quest is frankly Emersonian, an overt instance of American cultural nationalism. Unfortunately, *Kora*'s considerable verve and vivacity is shadowed by the immense power of James Joyce's *Ulysses*, still incomplete then, but appearing in magazine installments even as Williams wrote and read. Williams's use of mythology is essentially Joyce's, and to fight Joyce on any ground, let alone his prepared killing field, was beyond Williams's talents:

> Giants in the dirt. The gods, the Greek gods, smothered in filth and ignorance. The race is scattered over the world. Where is its home? Find it if you've the genius. Here Hebe with a sick jaw and a cruel husband,—her mother left no place for a brain to grow. Herakles rowing boats on Berry's Creek! Zeus is a country doctor without a taste for coin jingling. Supper is of a bastard nectar on rare nights for they will come—the rare nights! The ground lifts and out sally the heroes of Sophokles, of Æschylus. They go seeping down

into our hearts, they rain upon us and in the bog they sink again down through the white roots, down—to a saloon back of the railroad switch where they have that girl, you know, the one that should have been Venus by the lust that's in her. They've got her down there among the railroad men. A crusade couldn't rescue her. Up to jail—or call it down to Limbo—the Chief of Police our Pluto. It's all of the gods, there's nothing else worth writing of. They are the same men they always were—but fallen. Do they dance now, they that danced beside Helicon? They dance much as they did then, only, few have an eye for it, through the dirt and fumes.

The question becomes: who shall describe the dance of the gods as it is danced now in America? The answer is: Dr. Williams, who brings American babies into the world, and who sees exquisitely what we cannot see without him, which is how differently the gods come to dance here in America:

This is a slight stiff dance to a waking baby whose arms have been lying curled back above his head upon the pillow, making a flower—the eyes closed. Dead to the world! Waking is a little hand brushing away dreams. Eyes open. Here's a new world.

This dance figures again in the concluding improvisation of *Kora in Hell*, as an American seasonal rhythm akin to the natural year of Stevens's "Credences of Summer" and Emerson's "Experience":

Seeing the leaves dropping from the high and low branches the thought rises: this day of all others is the one chosen, all other days fall away from it on either side and only itself remains in perfect fullness. It is its own summer, of its leaves as they scrape on the smooth ground it must build its perfection. The gross summer of the year is only a halting counterpart of those fiery days of secret triumph which in reality themselves paint the year as if upon a parchment, giving each season a mockery of the warmth or frozenness which is within ourselves. The true seasons blossom or wilt not in fixed order but so that many of them may pass in a few weeks or hours whereas sometimes a whole life passes and the season remains of a piece from one end to the other.

The world is largest in the American summer, for Williams and Stevens, even as it was for their forefather, Emerson. *Spring and All* celebrates not this world, but the more difficult American skepticism of a hard spring, imperishably rendered in its magnificent opening lyric, "By the road to the contagious hospital," with its harsh splendor of inception, at once of vegetation, infants, and of Whitmanian or American poems:

> Lifeless in appearance, sluggish
> dazed spring approaches—
>
> They enter the new world naked,
> cold, uncertain of all
> save that they enter. All about them
> the cold, familiar wind—
>
> Now the grass, tomorrow
> the stiff curl of wildcarrot leaf
> One by one objects are defined—
> It quickens: clarity, outline of leaf
>
> But now the stark dignity of
> entrance—Still, the profound change
> has come upon them: rooted, they
> grip down and begin to awaken

The ancient fiction of the leaves, a continuous tradition from Homer and Virgil, through Dante and on to Spenser and Milton, Shelley and Whitman, receives one culmination in Stevens, and a very different apotheosis here in Williams. In the prose of *Spring and All*, Williams protests too emphatically that: "THE WORLD IS NEW," a protest that has been taken too much at its own self-mystifying evaluation by the most distinguished of the deconstructive critics of Williams, J. Hillis Miller and Joseph Riddel. But when the best poems in *Spring and All* unfold themselves, the reader can be persuaded that Williams has invented freshly the accurate metaphors for our American sense of imaginative belatedness: "There is / an approach with difficulty from / the dead—," and: "The rose is obsolete / but each petal ends in / an edge." Except for "By the road to the contagious hospital," the best poems in *Spring and All* are the justly famous ones: "The pure products of America / go crazy—," and "so much depends / upon / a red wheel / barrow."

More problematical are *The Great American Novel* and *The Descent of Winter*, pugnacious assaults upon Williams's own formal limits, yet assaults masked as ironies directed against the literary conventionalities of others. I prefer *The Descent of Winter*, where the authentic anxiety of belatedness, the only legitimate point of origin for any American literature, is expressed in relation to that most impossible of all influences, Shakespeare:

By writing he escaped from the world into the natural world of his mind. The unemployable world of his fine head was unnaturally useless in the gross exterior of his day—or any day. By writing he made this active. He melted himself into that grossness, and colored it with his powers. The proof that he was right and they passing, being that he continues always and naturally while their artificiality destroyed them. A man unable to employ himself in his world.

Therefore his seriousness and his accuracies, because it was not his play but the drama of his life. It is his anonymity that is baffling to nitwits and so they want to find an involved explanation—to defeat the plainness of the evidence.

When he speaks of fools he is one; when of kings he is one, doubly so in misfortune.

He is a woman, a pimp, a prince Hal—

Such a man is a prime borrower and standardizer—No inventor. He lives because he sinks back, does not go forward, sinks back into the mass—

He is Hamlet plainer than a theory—and in everything.

You can't buy a life again after it's gone, that's the way I mean.

He drinks awful bad and he beat me up every single month while I was carrying this baby, pretty nearly every week.

As an overview of Shakespeare, this is unquestionably the weakest commentary available since Tolstoy; but as a representation of Williams's dilemmas, it has a curious force, including the weird parody of Hemingway's agonistic stance in the last sentence I have just quoted. Despite his army of hyperbolic exegetes, Williams's nakedness in relation to the literary past is not so much that of "a new world naked" as it is that of a no longer so very new world awkwardly wrapped round by too many fine rags.

II

The best lyrics and Book I of *Paterson* are of a higher order, though they also betray darker anxieties of influence than even Williams's defiances dared to confront. They display also another kind of agon, the anxiety as to contemporary rivals, not so much Pound and Eliot as Wallace Stevens and Hart Crane, heirs to Keats and to Whitman, even as Williams was. No two readers are likely to agree upon just which shorter poems by Williams are his strongest, but the one that impresses and moves me most is "A Unison," where the title seems to comprehend most of the dictionary meanings of "unison": an identity of pitch in music; the same words spoken simultaneously by two or more speakers; musical parts combined in octaves; a concord, agreement, harmony. Thomas R. Whitaker, one of Williams's best and most sympathetic critics but no idolator, gives the best introduction to "A Unison":

> It is like an improvisation from *Kora in Hell*—but one with the quiet maturity of vision and movement that some three decades have brought. . . . As the implicit analogies and contrasts accumulate, we discover (long before the speaker tells us) that we are attending a "unison and a dance." This "death's festival"—*memento mori* and celebration of the "*Undying*"—evades neither the mystery of transience nor that of organic continuance, though neither can be "parsed" by the analytical mind. . . . In this composed testament of acceptance, Williams's saxifrage ("through metaphor to reconcile / the people and the stones") quietly does its work. . . . Not since Wordsworth has this natural piety been rendered so freshly and poignantly.

I would not wish to quarrel with Whitaker's judgment, yet there is very little Wordsworth and (inevitably) much Whitman and considerable Keats in "A Unison." Indeed, the poem opens with what must be called an echo from Whitman, in what I assume was a controlled allusion:

> The grass is very green, my friend,
> And tousled, like the head of —
> your grandson, yes?

We hear one of the uncanniest passages in Whitman, from *Song of Myself* 6:

> This grass is very dark to be from the white heads of old mothers,
> Darker than the colorless beards of old men,
> Dark to come from under the faint red roofs of mouths.

Whitman's great fantasia answers a child's question: "*What is the grass?*" As an Epicurean materialist, Whitman believed that the *what* was unknowable, but his remarkable troping on the grass takes a grand turn after his Homeric line: "And now it seems to me the beautiful uncut hair of graves." Williams simply borrows the trope, and even his "very green" merely follows Whitman's hint that a "very green" becomes a "very dark" color, in the shadow of mortality. "A Unison" insists upon:

> —what cannot be escaped: the
> mountain riding the afternoon as
> it does, the grass matted green,

> green underfoot and the air —
> rotten wood. *Hear! Hear them!*
> *the Undying.* The hill slopes away,
> then rises in the middleground,
> you remember, with a grove of gnarled
> maples centering the bare pasture,
> sacred, surely — for what reason?

Williams does not know whether he can or cannot say the reason, but the allusion is to Keats's characteristic, Saturnian shrine in *Hyperion*. For Williams it is "a shrine cinctured there by / the trees," the girdling effect suggested by the natural sculpture of Keats's shrine. Where Keats as the quester in *The Fall of Hyperion* pledges "all the mortals of the world, / And all the dead whose names are in our lips," and where Whitman insists, "The smallest sprout shows there is really no death," Williams neither salutes the living and the dead, nor folds the two into a single figuration. Rather, he *hears* and urges us to: "*Hear the unison of their voices.* . . ." How are we to interpret such an imaginative gesture? Are we hearing more, or enough more, than the unison of the voices of John Keats and Walt Whitman? Devoted Williamsites doubtless would reject the question, but it always retains its force, nevertheless. It is not less true of *The Waste Land* than it is of Williams. Eliot revises Whitman's "When Lilacs Last in the Dooryard Bloom'd" by fusing it with Tennyson (among others, but prime among those others). Image of voice or the trope of poetic identity then becomes a central problem.

Whitman once contrasted himself to Keats by rejecting "negative capability" and insisting instead that the great poet gave us the "powerful press of himself." Admirable as *Paterson* is (particularly its first book), does even it resolve the antithesis in Williams between his "objectivism" or negative capability, and his own, agonistic, powerful press of himself? Mariani ends his vast, idealizing biography by asserting that Williams established "an American poetic based on a new measure and a primary regard for the living, protean shape of the language as it was actually used." Hillis Miller, even more generously, tells us that Williams gave us a concept of poetry transcending both Homer and Wordsworth, both Aristotle and Coleridge:

> The word is given reality by the fact it names, but the independence of the fact from the word frees the word to be a fact in its own right and at the same time "dynamizes" it with meaning. The word can then carry the facts named in a new form into the realm of imagination.

Mariani and Miller are quite sober compared to more apocalyptic Williams-ites. Not even Whitman gave us "a new measure," and not Shakespeare himself freed a single word "to be a fact in its own right." William Carlos Williams was, at his best, a strong American poet, far better than his hordes of imitators. Like Ezra Pound's, Williams's remains a fairly problematical achievement in the traditions of American poetry. Some generations hence, it will become clear whether his critics have canonized him permanently, or subverted him by taking him too much at his own intentions. For now he abides, a live influence, and perhaps with even more fame to come.

LOUIS L. MARTZ

The Unicorn in Paterson

This is the first part of a long poem in four parts—that a man in himself is a city beginning, seeking, achieving and concluding his life in ways which the various aspects of a city may embody—if imaginatively conceived—any city, all the details of which may be made to voice his most intimate convictions. Part One introduces the elemental character of the place. The Second Part will comprise the modern replicas. Three will seek a language to make them vocal, and Four, the river below the falls, will be reminiscent of episodes— all that any one man may achieve in a lifetime.

So, in 1946, in his sixty-third year, Dr. Williams introduced the first part of his long poem *Paterson*, "a gathering up" of a lifetime's devotion to the poetical aim set for himself forty years before, when in his early poem, "The Wanderer," he dedicated his muse to "The Passaic, that filthy river."

> Then the river began to enter my heart,
> Eddying back cool and limpid
> Into the crystal beginning of its days.
> But with the rebound it leaped forward:
> Muddy, then black and shrunken
> Till I felt the utter depth of its rottenness . . .
> And dropped down knowing this was me now.
> But she lifted me and the water took a new tide
> Again into the older experiences,

From *Thought* 35, no. 139 (Winter 1960). © 1960 by Fordham University Press. Originally entitled "The Unicorn in *Paterson*: William Carlos Williams."

> And so, backward and forward,
> It tortured itself within me
> Until time had been washed finally under,
> And the river had found its level
> And its last motion had ceased
> And I knew all—it became me.

Steadily, tenaciously, amid the multifold demands of a medical career, the books of *Paterson* appeared: and in 1951 the promised four books stood complete, fulfilling the wanderer's goal, and carrying out exactly the four-part design announced in Book I.

No wonder, then, that some admirers of *Paterson* were struck with consternation and dismay, a few years later, at the news that a *fifth* book of *Paterson* was in progress! That four-part design, so carefully announced and explained by the poet on several occasions—was it to be discarded now? To say the least, the whole procedure was inconsiderate of those critics who had published careful explanations of the poem's symmetry—and encouraging to those other critics who had felt that Book IV did not fulfill the poem's brilliant beginning. But, as usual, Williams knew exactly what he was doing. When, in 1958, the threatened Book V at last appeared, it proved to be an epilogue or coda, considerably shorter than the other books, and written in a reminiscent mode that served to recapitulate and bind together all the foregoing poem. As Williams himself wrote on the dust jacket of Book V: "I had to take the world of Paterson into a new dimension if I wanted to give it imaginative validity. Yet I wanted to keep it whole, as it is to me."

The chief agent and symbol of that wholeness is one that may at first seem incongruous with Williams's lifetime dedication to the local, his persistent refusal to adopt or approve the learned, foreign allusions of Ezra Pound or T. S. Eliot: in Book V the organizing symbol is the series of matchless tapestries in The Cloisters representing *The Hunt of the Unicorn*. True, Williams had dealt briefly with these tapestries in the third book of *Paterson*:

> A tapestry hound
> with his thread teeth drawing crimson from
> the throat of the unicorn

But there the allusion to the world of traditional art seemed ironically overwhelmed by the surrounding scenes of basement ugliness and the fighting between "the guys from Paterson" and "the guys from Newark." Literally, it is only a short drive from Paterson to The Cloisters—but the gap of nearly five hundred years, the distance from France to the Passaic—these are dimensions strange to Williams, however familiar they may be to Pound or Eliot. But an afternoon

spent with the great tapestries will show once more the canniness and subtlety of
Williams's poetical strategies in *Paterson*.

Williams is defending and explaining his own technique by suggesting an
analogy with the mode of the tapestries; and however unlikely any similarity
may at first appear, the essential kinship is truly there. For these tapestries, like
Paterson, achieve their success through a peculiar combination of the local and
the mythical. We have the one hundred and one trees, shrubs, herbs, and flowers
so realistically woven that eighty-five of them have been identified by botanists
and praised for the exactitude of their reproduction; the "millefleurs background"
is not composed of merely symbolical designs, but the colors burst forth from
the actual, recognizable violet, cornflower, daisy, calendula, or dandelion. Yet all
this actuality serves to border and center the mythical beast of oriental legend,
serves to enfold and surround the human figures, the dogs, birds, and wild beasts,
the castles and streams, the spears and hunting horns that crowd the scenes with
a happy disregard of perspective—even to the point where the sixth tapestry
superimposes the wounding of the unicorn upon an upper corner of the larger
scene where the mythical beast is presented dead before the King and Queen.
Meanwhile, amid the brilliant distortions of art and the splendor of color in
flowers and costume, we find the brutal faces of certain varlets, the dog gutted by
the unicorn's horn, the dog biting the unicorn's back, the vicious spears stabbing
the "milk-white beast," the slanting, provocative, betraying eyes of the female
attendant upon the virgin.

>   .   cyclamen, columbine, if the art
>   with which these flowers have been
>   put down is to be trusted—and
>   again oak leaves and twigs
>   that brush the deer's antlers   .   .
>   the brutish eyes of the deer
>   not to be confused
>   with the eyes of the Queen
>   are glazed with death   .
>   .   a rabbit's rump escaping
>   through the thicket   .
>
>   a tapestry
>   silk and wool shot with silver threads
>   a milk-white one horned beast
>   I, Paterson, the King-self
>   saw the lady
>   through the rough woods
>   outside the palace walls

                    among the stench of sweating horses
                            and gored hounds
                                    yelping with pain
                    the heavy breathing pack
                            to see the dead beast
                                    brought in at last
                    across the saddle bow
                            among the oak trees.

The placing of that line, "I, Paterson, the King-self," implies a parallel
between "Paterson," the poet, man, self, and city of the poem, and the Unicorn.
The mythical beast is the spirit of the imagination, the immortal presence of art:

                    The Unicorn
            has no match
                    or mate   .   the artist
                            has no peer   .
        .   .   .   .

            So through art alone, male and female, a field of
            flowers, a tapestry, spring flowers unequaled
            in loveliness.
                    through this hole
                    at the bottom of the cavern
                    of death, the imagination
                    escapes intact
            .   he bears a collar round his neck
                    hid in the bristling hair.

Thus in the last of the series, the most famous of the tapestries, the Unicorn
appears in peaceful resurrection. So "Paterson" now writes "In old age"—the
opening line of Book V—and knows the threat of mortality as well as the re-
assurance promised by everything that the Unicorn represents—as we learn from
the long closing passage dominated by the tapestries:

                    —the aging body
                            with the deformed great-toe nail
                    makes itself known
                            coming
                                    to search me out—with a
                                    rare smile
                    among the thronging flowers of that field
                            where the Unicorn
                                    is penned by a low

wooden fence
     in April!

the cranky violet
    like a knight in chess,
        the cinque-foil,
yellow faced—
      this is a French
         or Flemish tapestry—
the sweetsmelling primrose
      growing close to the ground, that poets
      have made famous in England,
        I cannot tell it all:
slippered flowers
      crimson and white,
         balanced to hang
on slender bracts, cups evenly arranged upon a stem,
      fox glove, the eglantine
        or wild rose,
pink as a lady's ear lobe when it shows
      beneath the hair,
          campanella, blue and purple tufts
small as forget-me-not among the leaves.
      Yellow centers, crimson petals
        and the reverse,
dandelion, love-in-a-mist,
    corn flowers,
      thistle and others
the names and perfumes I do not know.
      The woods are filled with holly
        (I have told you, this
is a fiction, pay attention),
        the yellow flag of the French fields is here
         and a congeries of other flowers
as well: daffodils
     and gentian, the daisy, columbine
       petals
myrtle, dark and light
    and calendulas .

Anyone who reads the excellent pamphlet on the flora of the tapestries provided by the museum will see at once that most of the flowers here included

by Williams are clearly recognizable and listed under these names; but the poet is
not presenting a catalogue: he is recreating the act of personal, immediate, imaginative apprehension. Thus at times the poet gives his own familiar names, draws
his own conclusions, imagines likenesses. The "myrtle, dark and light," for instance, must be the "periwinkle (*Vinca*)" which "appears only in the two normal
colors of white and blue." And the "cinque-foil, / yellow faced" is not mentioned
in the museum's account, but it is not hard to find it suggested by certain flowers.
Most important, the familiar, intimate quality of the poet's account reminds us
that many of these flowers have appeared in the dozens of flower-poems and the
hundreds of flower-images scattered throughout the poetry of William Carlos
Williams, from his early tributes to the daisy, the primrose, and the "yellow
cinquefoil," down through the great tribute to Demuth, "The Crimson Cycla-
men," and on into the recent long flower-tribute to his wife: *Asphodel, That
Greeny Flower*, where the poet recalls his boyhood collection of "pressed flowers."
Williams is one of the great poets of flowers and foliage, which he observes and
represents with a loving and a scientific accuracy akin to that of the Unicorn
tapestries. Indeed, in a passage typical of *Paterson*'s mode of organization, this
fifth book itself reminds us from the outset of the poet's personal love of flowers
by including on its fourth page a personal letter to "Dear Bill":

> I wish you and F. could have come. It was a grand day and we missed
> you two, one and all missed you. Forgetmenot, wild columbine, white
> and purple violets, white narcissus, wild anemonies and yards and
> yards of delicate wild windflowers along the brook showed up at
> their best. . . .

> How lovely to read your memories of the place; a place is made of
> them as well as the world around it. Most of the flowers were put in
> many years ago and thrive each spring, the wild ones in some new
> spot that is exciting to see. Hepaticas and bloodroot are now all over
> the place, and the trees that were infants are now tall creatures filled
> this season with orioles, some rare warbler like the Myrtle and mag-
> nolia warblers and a wren has the best nest in the garage.

So the new Book V suggests that we might regard *Paterson* as a kind
of tapestry, woven out of memories and observations, composed by one man's
imagination, but written in part by his friends, his patients, and all the milling
populace of Paterson, past and present; letters from Williams's friends are scattered amply throughout the poem: Book V devotes a whole page to transcribing
a letter from Ezra Pound.

The whole, as Williams insists, is a "fiction" ("pay attention"), but it is at
the same time a personal testament to the poet's vehement belief "that there is a

source *in America* for everything we think or do." Why, then, he asks, "Why should I move from this place / where I was born?" —Rutherford, New Jersey, next door to Paterson.

II

To find the source, to discover the place—in America—has been his life-long aim. Thus we have heard now for about forty years Williams's warm, friendly, admiring, generous disagreement with the poetical directions of his life-long friend Ezra Pound ("The best enemy United States verse has," he once declared). And so too, in quite a different tone, we have heard Williams's rasping antagonism toward the achievement of T. S. Eliot. The publication of *The Waste Land*, he declares in his *Autobiography*, was "the great catastrophe to our letters":

> There was heat in us, a core and a drive that was gathering headway upon the theme of a rediscovery of a primary impetus, the elementary principle of all art, in the local conditions. Our work staggered to a halt for a moment under the blast of Eliot's genius which gave the poem back to the academics. We did not know how to answer him.

> Critically Eliot returned us to the classroom just at the moment when I felt that we were on the point of an escape to matters much closer to the essence of a new art form itself—rooted in the locality which should give it fruit. . . .

> If with his skill he could have been kept here to be employed by our slowly shaping drive, what strides might we not have taken! . . . By his walking out on us we were stopped, for the moment, cold. It was a bad moment. Only now, as I predicted, have we begun to catch hold again.

In those words, published in the same year as the fourth book of *Paterson*, we have a clue to one aspect of that poem's whole design. The more we read and reread *Paterson*, the more it emerges as a subtly devised protest against the cosmopolitan, the learned, the foreign aspects of such poems as *The Waste Land*, *Four Quartets*, and *The Cantos*. This is made especially plain near the end of the first book of *Paterson*, where Williams writes:

> Moveless
> he envies the men that ran
> and could run off

toward the peripheries—
to other centers, direct—
for clarity (if
they found it)
                loveliness and
authority in the world—

a sort of springtime
toward which their minds aspired
but which he saw,
within himself—ice bound

and leaped, "the body, not until
the following spring, frozen in
an ice cake."

It is a leap from the Falls: one of the major symbols of the poem; and whether or not the poet, like old Sam Patch, the daring diver, perishes at the river's bottom, the descent must be made:

Caught (in mind)
beside the water he looks down, listens!
But discovers, still, no syllable in the confused
uproar: missing the sense (though he tries)
untaught but listening, shakes with the intensity
of his listening.

It is a descent, through memory, to the sources of the self, as Williams makes clear in a passage from the second book of *Paterson*—a passage that later appeared as the opening poem of his collection *The Desert Music* (1954):

The descent beckons
        as the ascent beckoned.
                Memory is a kind
of accomplishment,
        a sort of renewal
                even
an initiation, since the spaces it opens are new places
        inhabited by hordes
                heretofore unrealized,
of new kinds—
        since their movements
                are towards new objectives
(even though formerly they were abandoned)

Thus *Paterson* becomes the full realization of the moral vision, the literary theory, the aesthetic manifesto, set forth in the best of his earlier works, *In the American Grain* (1925). We must not mistake this book for an interpretation of history, although it deals with Montezuma, de Soto, Raleigh, Daniel Boone, and George Washington, and although it contains excerpts from the journals of Columbus and from the writings of Cotton Mather, Ben Franklin, and John Paul Jones. The point is not history but rather a search in the memory of America to discover, to invent, symbols of the ideals from which Williams's life and writings have developed.

In the American Grain works with American figures, but the basic issues of the book are universal. It seeks a way of moving from an old world into a new; it seeks a way of leaving the finished forms of culture and dealing with the roar, the chaos, of the still-to-be-achieved. The book discerns two modes of treating the problem. One is found in Williams's version of the Puritan, who represents here, not a single religious creed, but the way of all men who lack "the animate touch," and who therefore set up within themselves a "resistance to the wilderness" which is the new life all about them.

In contrast to this view, with "its rigid clarity, its *inhuman* clarity, its steel-like thrust from the heart of each isolate man straight into the tabernacle of Jehovah," Williams presents another vision, dramatized by a group of great explorers, sensitive to the wonder of the life all about them in the new world. There is Columbus, who on the twelfth of October found a world that was filled with things "wonderful," "handsome," "marvelous," "beautiful." "During that time I walked among the trees which was the most beautiful thing which I had ever seen. . . ." They are the very words which twenty-five years later Williams recalls in the fourth book of *Paterson*, thus picking up the phrase "beautiful thing" which has formed the theme of his poem's third book. And we have Cortéz, Ponce de Leon, de Soto, Raleigh, and Champlain, "like no one else about him, watching, keeping the thing whole within him with almost a woman's tenderness—but such an energy for detail—a love of the exact detail—."

In these explorers Williams finds a quality of wonder utterly different from what is found in Cotton Mather's "Wonders of the Invisible World," his defense of the Salem witchcraft trials, from which Williams here provides long extracts. In Cotton Mather's own words, the Puritans "embraced a voluntary Exile in a squallid, horrid American Desart"; they felt themselves "a People of God settled in those, which were once the *Devil's* Territories." *In the American Grain* then turns from these accounts of witchcraft to a chapter entitled "Père Sebastian Rasles," but sixteen pages pass before we meet this missionary to the Indians of Maine. Instead we are moved abruptly from Cotton Mather to the Parisian world of the 1920s, where we find Williams surrounded by Picasso, Gertrude Stein, the Prince of Dahomi, James and Norah Joyce, Bryher, H. D., "dear Ezra," and other expatriates. Williams is discussing with Valéry Larbaud the situation of the American writer. "What we are," he argues, "has its origin in what *the nation* in the past has been . . . unless everything that is, proclaim a ground on which it stand, it has no worth . . . what has been morally, aesthetically worth while in America has rested upon peculiar and discoverable ground." And in that ground, he declares, we find "two flaming doctrines." One is Williams's version of the Puritan, and the other is that represented by Rasles, who here becomes a symbol of a way of life maintained by the animate touch. For thirty-four years, says Williams, this French Jesuit lived among his Indians, "*touching* them every day." In Rasles Williams discovers "a spirit, rich, blossoming, generous, able to give and to receive, full of taste, a nose, a tongue, a laugh, enduring, self-forgetful in beneficence—a new spirit in the New World." His vision of life as imagined by Williams is one the poet can share: "Nothing shall be ignored. All shall be included. The world is parcel of the Church so that every leaf, every vein in every leaf, the throbbing of the temples is of that mysterious flower. Here is richness, here is color, here is form." "Reading his letters, it is a river that brings sweet water to us. *This* is a moral source not reckoned with, peculiarly sensitive and daring in its close embrace of native things."

What does it all mean set thus in Paris, amid exiles gathered from England, Africa, Spain, Ireland, and especially America? These exiles, it seems, must be a modern version of the Puritans. They are those who have felt themselves living in a "squallid, horrid American Desart"; they have refused, like Cotton Mather, to embrace the wilderness. Williams turns instead to those like Daniel Boone, who, says Williams, "lived to enjoy ecstasy through his single devotion to the wilderness with which he was surrounded"; like Rasles, Boone sought "to explore always more deeply, to see, to feel, to touch. . . ." For Williams, the trouble with modern American culture is that the meaning of life has been obscured "by a field of unrelated culture stuccoed upon it," obscured by what he calls "the aesthetic adhesions of the present day." He seeks instead the "impact of the bare soul upon the very twist of the fact which is our world about us." For in this impact, the poet (in us all) discovers or invents the beautiful thing. True, the new world no longer holds "the orchidean beauty" that Cortéz, "overcome with wonder," saw in Montezuma's Mexico: "Streets, public squares, markets, temples, palaces, the city spread its dark life upon the earth of a new world, rooted there, sensitive to its richest beauty, but so completely removed from those foreign contacts which harden and protect, that at the very breath of conquest it vanished." True, we have instead the city—Paterson—that has resulted from the schemes of Alexander Hamilton: "Paterson he wished to make capital of the country because there was waterpower there which to his time and mind seemed colossal. And so he organized a company to hold the land thereabouts, with dams and sluices, the origin today of the vilest swillhole in christendom, the

Passaic River . . ." For all this, Williams argues, we must still, like Boone and Houston, make "a descent to the ground" of our desire. "However hopeless it may seem, we have no other choice: we must go back to the beginning. . . ."

III

From this bare ground Williams then begins his *Paterson*; an answer to those "who know all the Latin and some of the Sanskrit names" [*In the American Grain*]. Williams prepares his answer in a way subtly suggested by a passage in the second book of *Paterson*, where he seems to echo wryly one of the most famous passages of Pound, Canto 45, on usury, where Pound adopts the manner of a medieval or a renaissance preacher:

> With usura hath no man a house of good stone
> each block cut smooth and well fitting
> that design might cover their face,
> with usura
> hath no man a painted paradise on his church wall
> *harpes et luthes*
> . . . .
> with usura the line grows thick
> with usura is no clear demarcation
> and no man can find site for his dwelling.
> Stone cutter is kept from his stone
> weaver is kept from his loom
> . . . .
> Came not by usura Angelico; came not Ambrogio Praedis,
> Came no church of cut stone signed: *Adamo me fecit*
> . . . .
> Usura rusteth the chisel
> It rusteth the craft and the craftsman
> It gnaweth the thread in the loom
> None learneth to weave gold in her pattern

And now this from *Paterson*:

> Without invention nothing is well spaced,
> unless the mind change, unless
> the stars are new measured, according
> to their relative positions, the
> line will not change . . .
> . . . .

>   . . . without invention
> nothing lies under the witch-hazel
> bush, the alder does not grow from among
> the hummocks margining the all
> but spent channel of the old swale,
> the small foot-prints
> of the mice under the overhanging
> tufts of the bunch-grass will not
> appear: without invention the line
> will never again take on its ancient
> divisions when the word, a supple word,
> lived in it, crumbled now to chalk.

What does this contrast say of these two poets at their best? Williams's own critical acuteness gives us the answer in one of his letters of 1932:

> So far I believe that Pound's line in his *Cantos*—there is something *like* what we shall achieve. Pound in his mould, a medieval inspiration, patterned on a substitution of medieval simulacra for a possible, not yet extant modern and living material, has made a precomposition for us. Something which when later (perhaps) packed and realized in living, breathing stuff will (in its changed form) be the thing.

It is a summary of Williams's achievement in *Paterson*: the mold is Pound's, combining verse and prose; the line is Pound's, with its flexible cadences, breaking the pentameter; but everything is altered through Williams's invention, his conviction that bold exploration of the local will result in the discovery of a new world blossoming all about him. Pound's mind lives at its best among the splendors of ancient human artifacts, and when these splendors seem threatened, Pound seeks a social answer. He seeks to make art possible by reforming the economic basis of society. It is a difference between the two friends that Pound has acutely described in his essay on Williams (1928), as he contrasts their two temperaments: "If he wants to 'do' anything about what he sees, this desire for action does not rise until he has meditated in full and at leisure. Where I see scoundrels and vandals, he sees a spectacle or an ineluctable process of nature. Where I want to kill at once, he ruminates."

At the same time, in his ruminative way, Williams gradually implies some degree of sympathy with Pound's economic views. Among the prose passages of the second book of *Paterson*, we find attacks on the Federal Reserve System; we find, too, implied attacks on Alexander Hamilton's plans for federal financing and for creating a great "National Manufactory" powered by the Passaic falls.

These prose excerpts on financial matters are interwoven with the poetical sermon of the evangelist who, in the second book of *Paterson*, delivers his sermon against money to the birds and trees of the park. But this financial theme, thus introduced, is tightly contained within this section: it lies there dormant, recessive, exerting a tacit pressure on the landscape, until, in the center of Book IV, it bursts out again in a highly Poundian diatribe beginning "Money: Joke." Here is a section composed in something like Pound's broken multi-cultural style, with expressions in Hebrew, Spanish, and German, along with very crude American slang; and including too some allusions to the Parthenon, Phidias, and Pallas Athene—all this ending with an overt echo of Pound's unmistakable epistolary style:

> IN
> venshun.
> O.KAY
> In venshun

(It sounds like Pound nodding his head to the passage on invention that I have just quoted.)

> and seeinz az how yu hv / started. Will you consider
> a remedy of a lot:
>> i.e. LOCAL control of local purchasing
>>> power   .
>>>>   ?   ?
> Difference between squalor of spreading slums
> and splendor of renaissance cities.

It is a tribute to Pound, yes; but it is not for Williams to conclude his own poem in this foreign vein, it is not for Williams to excoriate the present and celebrate the "splendor of renaissance cities." This is an invitation that Williams has already refused to accept in the third book of *Paterson*, entitled "The Library," where we find the poet attempting to discover a "sanctuary to our fears" amid the "cool of books":

> A cool of books
> will sometimes lead the mind to libraries
> of a hot afternoon, if books can be found
> cool to the sense to lead the mind away.

He is attempting to escape from the roar of that Falls which provides the central symbol of this poem, for the roar of the Falls in his mind, "pouring down," has left him exhausted.

>   a falls unseen
>   tumbles and rights itself
>   and refalls—and does not cease, falling
>   and refalling with a roar, a reverberation
>   not of the falls but of its rumor
>   unabated.

Here, the mysterious evocative symbol of the great Falls of the Passaic comes as close to clarity as we shall ever find it. It seems to represent the roar of human speech, the roar of human thought in the mind; it is the roar of the language coming down from the past, mingling with the present, and now bursting downward over the brain of "Paterson," who seeks to find somehow in that fall of speech, the beautiful thing that is the ground of his desire. "What do I do? I listen, to the water falling. . . . This is my entire occupation." But now he is

>   Spent from wandering the useless
>   streets these months, faces folded against
>   him like clover at nightfall,

and he feels that somehow

>   Books will give rest sometimes against
>   the uproar of water falling
>   and righting itself to refall filling
>   the mind with its reverberation.

But it is not so. As he sits there reading "old newspaper files," old annals of Paterson—things like those prose passages of which his poem is in part compounded—as he reads, he finds the roar there, too: stories of fire, cyclone and flood that now beset the poet until his mind "reels, starts back amazed from the reading"—until the very poem threatens to break apart upon the page. Where to turn? What to do? In ironical answer, Williams brings in certain excerpts from a letter headed "S. Liz," that is, from St. Elizabeth's Hospital:

>   re   read *all* the Gk tragedies in
>   Loeb.—plus Frobenius, plus Gesell.
>   plus Brooks Adams
>   ef you ain't read him all.—
>   Then Golding's Ovid is in
>   Everyman's lib.
>
>   & nif you want a readin
>   list ask papa—but don't
>   go rushin to *read* a book

> just cause it is mentioned
> eng passang — is fraugs.

Williams's answer to Pound is sly. On the next page, he prints an excerpt from some record evidently found in the Paterson Library concerning the drillings taken at the artesian well of the Passaic Rolling Mill, Paterson, and as the results of this local rock-drill run down the page, the excerpt concludes with this significant suggestion: "The fact that the rock salt of England, and of some of the other salt mines of Europe, is found in rocks of the same age as this, raises the question whether it may not also be found here."

"Whether it may not also be found here." For Williams, it may, it can, it will be found here, as he proves by giving in the final section of Book IV a recovery of the source: the pastoral Paterson of early days at peace with the Falls.

> In a deep-set valley between hills, almost hid
> by dense foliage lay the little village.
> Dominated by the Falls the surrounding country
> was a beautiful wilderness where mountain pink
> and wood violet throve: a place inhabited only
> by straggling trappers and wandering Indians.

> Just off Gun Mill yard, on the gully
> was a long rustic winding stairs leading
> to a cliff on the opposite side of the river.
> At the top was Fyfield's tavern — watching
> the birds flutter and bathe in the little
> pools in the rocks formed by the falling
> mist — of the Falls.

Here is our home, says the poet, inland by the Falls and not in the outgoing sea, as Williams concludes in the rousing finale of Book IV:

> I warn you, the sea is *not* our home.
>   the sea is not our home.

Here the sea appears to symbolize something more than simple death, national or personal annihilation. For this is also a sea where "float words, snaring the seeds":

> the nostalgic sea
> sopped with our cries
>   Thalassa! Thalassa!
> calling us home   .
> I say to you, Put wax rather in your

> ears against the hungry sea
> > it is not our home!
> .   draws us in to drown, of losses
> and regrets   .

The sea appears to represent the pull of longing toward a lost culture, a pull outward from the source, as he goes on to indicate by an overwrought cry that seems to parody the longing of a Pound or an Eliot:

> Oh that the rocks of the Areopagus had
> kept their sounds, the voices of the law!
> Or that the great theatre of Dionysius
> could be aroused by some modern magic
>
> .   .   .   .
>
> Thalassa! Thalassa!
> > Drink of it, be drunk!
> > > Thalassa
> immaculata: our home, our nostalgic
> mother in whom the dead, enwombed again
> cry out to us to return   .

". . . not our home!" cries the poet again in violent protest, "It is NOT our home." And suddenly at the very close of this fourth book, the scene shifts, the tone shifts, to a common seashore with a man bathing in the sea, and his dog waiting for him on the beach.

> When he came out, lifting his knees
> through the waves she went to him frisking
> her rump awkwardly   .
> Wiping his face with his hand he turned
> to look back to the waves, then
> knocking at his ears, walked up
> to stretch out flat on his back in
> the hot sand   .

And finally after a brief nap and a quick dressing, the man

> > turned again
> to the water's steady roar, as of a distant
> waterfall   .   Climbing the
> bank, after a few tries, he picked
> some beach plums from a low bush and
> sampled one of them, spitting the seed out,
> then headed inland, followed by the dog.

"Headed inland"—here at the very close, Williams echoes once again his prose preparation for this poem, *In the American Grain*, for in the closing pages of that earlier book, he had used the same phrasing to describe the achievement of Edgar Allan Poe. "His greatness," Williams there declared, "is in that he turned his back" upon everything represented by a Longfellow and "faced inland, to originality, with the identical gesture of a Boone." And indeed Williams's account here of Poe's method in his tales is perhaps the best account of *Paterson* that we have yet received:

> the significance and the secret is: authentic particles, a thousand of which spring to the mind for quotation, taken apart and reknit with a view to emphasize, enforce and make evident, the *method*. Their quality of skill in observation, their heat, local verity, being *overshadowed* only by the detached, the abstract, the cold philosophy of their joining together; a method springing so freshly from the local conditions which determine it, by their emphasis of firm crudity and lack of coordinated structure, as to be worthy of most painstaking study—.

So the two major works of William Carlos Williams reinforce each other, while the tapestry of *Paterson* recalls the whole body of Williams's poetry, as now six pages from the end of Book V we hear:

> "the river has returned to its beginnings"
>   and backward
>   (and forward)
>   it tortures itself within me
>   until time has been washed finally under:
>   and "I knew all (or enough)
>   it became me   .   "

J. HILLIS MILLER

Williams: Poet of Reality

As he opened his eyes, he found himself alone, lying in a comfortable place among the trees, quite in the open, with torn branches on all sides of him and leaves, ripped from their hold, plastered in fragments upon the rocks about him. Unfortunately, though, he didn't recognize the place. No one was there to inform him of his whereabouts and when he did begin to encounter passers-by, they didn't even understand, let alone speak his language. He could recall nothing of the past.

In this text alone of his mature work does Williams describe the state of deprivation which was his starting point. It appears only once because it was so soon transcended. The poet does not become himself, nor is his writing possible, until he has gone beyond it. Only in Williams's first published work, the *Poems* of 1909, that pastiche of the romantic motifs he was soon to reject, is there an echo of the experience here described:

> But now among low plains or banks which rear
> Their flower hung screens o'erhead I wander—where?
> These fields I know not; know not whence I come;
>
> Nor aught of all which spreads so touching near.
> The very bird-songs I have heard them n'er
> And this strange folk they know not e'en my name.

From *Poets of Reality*. © 1965 by the President and Fellows of Harvard College. The Belknap Press, 1965. Originally entitled "William Carlos Williams."

The young man who found himself alone in a strange land was the hero of a long narrative poem, modeled on Keats's *Endymion*, which Williams wrote during his medical training, at about the same time that he was writing the poems published in the slender volume of 1909. Though he added more and more scenes to the poem, it remained unfinished. The poem told the story of a young prince taken from his bride at the wedding feast, before the consummation of his marriage, and transported to a strange country. His wanderings were described as he attempted to recover his past and find his way home again.

The young prince's state of loss was complete. It was the exact antithesis of the condition presupposed in Williams's work after the *Poems* of 1909. Instead of belonging to the place where he found himself, he did not even recognize it. He was detached from his familiar surroundings, like a leaf torn from its tree and cast on the bare rocks of an alien earth. He could not remember the past, when he was married to his locality and invested with all its privileges. He saw the present scene across an empty space, as something strange and unrecognizable, and what he beheld was fragmented, broken branches and torn leaves, the relics of some inexplicable disaster.

The prince was also bereft of language and cut off from other people. These two losses are intertwined. Language is the chief means by which human beings know one another and transform a place into a culture. The prince could not understand the passers-by, nor they him, and so he was forced to endure a terrifying alienation, like that of Yanko Goorall in Conrad's "Amy Foster." A private language is no language, for the essence of language is its use as a means of communication.

Words also join a man to the physical world. The collective naming of flower, tree, rock, and bird brings them into existence for a people, and assimilates them into a culture, giving them a measure, a meaning, and a place. "The only means [man] has to give value to life," says Williams, "is to recognise it with the imagination and name it." Naming and imagining are the same. They are that originating act which creates a culture by "the lifting of an environment to expression." The prince was without a local culture, and therefore he could not recognize the place where he was. His failure to speak the language of the country made him a naked consciousness confronting a world in fragments inhabited by a people speaking words without meaning to him. It is no wonder that he "went on, homeward or seeking a home that was his own."

The poet was unable to bring his prince to his native land, and therefore the poem remained unfinished, a potentially endless series of episodes, never accomplishing the leap between homelessness and home. His next long poem, "The Wanderer," comes first in *The Collected Earlier Poems*. It celebrates the homecoming which makes his poetry possible. Here the marriage of the prince is consummated at last. An important letter to Marianne Moore provides the terms in which this homecoming can be understood. The poet praises Miss Moore for recognizing the "inner security" which is the basis of his work. That security, he says, "is something which occurred once when I was about twenty, a sudden resignation to existence, a despair—if you wish to call it that, but a despair which made everything a unit and at the same time a part of myself. I suppose it might be called a sort of nameless religious experience. I resigned, I gave up" [*Selected Letters*, ed. John Thirlwall (New York: McDowell, Obolensky, 1957); all further references to this text will be abbreviated as *SL*]. He abandoned his private consciousness, that hollow bubble in the midst of the solidity of the world. The resulting "anonymity" is assumed in all his work and recurrently affirmed there, as when Paterson, the man-city, asks: "Why even speak of 'I,' . . . which / interests me almost not at all?" To give up the ego means to give up also those dramas of the interchange of subject and object, self and world, which have long been central in Western philosophy and literature. The poet's resignation puts him beyond romanticism. He reaches at the age of twenty the place which Wallace Stevens attains only after decades of struggle to harmonize imagination and reality. After his resignation there is always and everywhere only one realm. Consciousness permeates the world, and the world has entered into the mind. It is "an identity—it can't be / otherwise—an / interpenetration, both ways" [*Paterson* (New York: New Directions, 1963); all further references to this text will be abbreviated as *P*].

Williams's work expresses, quietly and without fanfare, a revolution in human sensibility. When he gives himself up to the world he gives up the coordinates and goals which had polarized earlier literature. Romantic poetry, like idealist philosophy, had been based on an opposition between the inner world of the subject and the outer world of things. Since the world is other than the self, that self can ground itself on something external. This tradition remains valid through the nineteenth and early twentieth centuries, down to Yeats and the early Stevens. In Williams it disappears. This is perhaps most apparent, to a reader steeped in romanticism, in a strange lack of tension in his work. Gone are both the profound abysses of subjectivity, so important in earlier poetry, and the limitless dimensions of the external world, through which Shelley's Alastor or Browning's Paracelsus sought a vanishing presence and strained every nerve to reach it. "How foolish to seek new worlds," says Williams, ". . . when we must know that any world warmed by the arts will surpass the very Elysian Fields if the imagination reaches its end there" ["Introduction" to Byron Vazakas, *Transfigured Night* (New York: The Macmillan Company, 1946)]. Only in the *Poems* of 1909 does the image of fathomless space appear, the "soundless infinite blue day," and only there are found examples of the romantic theme of an unattainable presence in the landscape, as in the assertion that poetry will take the reader "to worlds afar whose fruits all anguish mend," or in the last lines of "To Simplicity" [from *Poems* (Rutherford, N.J.: privately printed, 1909); all further references to this text will be abbreviated as *P* (1909)]:

> Hark! Hark! Mine ears are numb
> With dread! Methought a faint hallooing rang!
> Where art thou hid? Cry, cry again! I come!
> I come! I come!

In Williams's mature work, if something exists at all, it dwells in the only realm there is, a space both subjective and objective, a region of copresence in which anywhere is everywhere, and all times are one time. "What is time but an impertinence?" asks the poet [*The Great American Novel* (Paris: Contact, 1923); all further references to this text will be abbreviated as *GAN*]. Since there are no distances there is "no direction" [*P*], no reason to go one way rather than another because there is no reason to go anywhere at all. To be in one place is already to be in all other places. "I won't follow causes," he says. "I can't. The reason is that it seems so much more important to me that I *am*. Where shall one go? What shall one do?" [*SL*]. Byron Vazakas is an authentic American poet because he "hasn't had 'to go anywhere.' There he is . . . anywhere, therefore *here*, for his effects. And being here, he sees here; and hears here."

This situation means the disappearance of another characteristic of traditional philosophy and poetry: thinking in terms of causality. Western thought has been dominated since Aristotle by the idea of cause, whether this has meant a search for the ground of things in some transcendent being, or whether it has meant conceiving of nature as a chain of cause and effect, each element pushing the next in an endless series. Both kinds of causality vanish in Williams's work. All things exist simultaneously in one realm, and though they may interact they are not related causally. The idea of causal sequence is replaced by the notion of a poetry which "lives with an intrinsic movement of its own to verify its authenticity" [*Selected Essays* (New York: Random House, 1954); all further references to this text will be abbreviated as *SE*]. As in other areas of contemporary thought, linear determinism gives way to a system of reciprocal motions, "intrinsic, undulant, a physical more than a literary character" [*SE*].

It is appropriate that Keats should have been the poet who most influenced Williams in his youth, for Williams might be said to begin where Keats ends. The leap into things which Keats accomplishes by the most extreme reach of the sympathetic imagination is achieved by Williams at the beginning, and attained also is that perpetual present which is expressed in the epigraph adapted from the "Ode on a Grecian Urn" which the poet puts on the title page of his first book: "Happy melodist forever piping songs forever new." "I quit Keats," he says, "just at the moment he himself did—with Hyperion's scream" [*The Autobiography of William Carlos Williams* (New York: Random House, 1951)]. Williams means of course Apollo's scream. Keats's poetry reaches its climax with Apollo's attainment of immortal knowledge. With that climax it melts into the silence beyond poetry. Williams's work begins with the muteness of what he calls in *Spring and All* an "approximate co-extension with the universe."

This silence will provide another definition of the place Williams enters when he resigns himself to existence. The romantic or idealist tradition in one way or another presupposes a separation of words from things. Words are instruments which the poet may use to reach and grapple objects in order to close the gap between himself and them. Through words the poet imposes his will on things and so transforms them. The naming of poetry is the creation of a cunning verbal replica which changes things into spiritualized stuff and so assimilates them into the mind. The idea that words "represent" things is deeply a part of the tradition of metaphysical thinking of which romanticism is a version. Williams never uses words in this way. For him things are already possessed before being named. When he gives up he reaches a place which is before language: "Things have no names for me and places have no significance" [*SL*]. This loss of language is radically different from the aphasia of the prince in the early poem. The prince's mutism expressed his separation from other people and the land. Now all things have been assimilated and the need for words has disappeared. If language is the voice of consciousness in its isolation, union with everything can be reached only by leaving it behind. "As a reward for this anonymity," says Williams, "I feel as much a part of things as trees and stones" [*SL*]. His new speechlessness is the silence which follows Apollo's scream. In it he belongs to "a wordless / world / without personality" [*The Collected Earlier Poems* (New York: New Directions, 1951); all further references to this text will be abbreviated as *CEP*].

If trees, flowers, mountains, and meadows are for Wordsworth and Tennyson the dwelling places of a haunting presence, other romantic poets describe the search for a similar ideal incarnated successively in the women they love. To Gérard de Nerval all women are the same woman, and with each is experienced a failure to possess the ideal: "La Treizième revient . . . C'est encore la première; / Et c'est toujours la seule." This theme too no longer has meaning for Williams. If everything is part of himself this includes men and women. The strangers speaking an alien tongue in his early poem are replaced by the men and women of *Paterson*. The latter exist within the man-city and are the poet's mind incarnated: "Inside the bus one sees / his thoughts sitting and standing. His / thoughts alight and scatter" [P]. In the same way he says of one of the personae of *The Great American Novel*, a "savior of the movies": "his great heart had expanded so as to include the whole city." This expansion is anticipated in the last text in the *Poems* of 1909, where the poet affirms that with the help of "Perfection" he has transcended the "profusion / Of space" and "o'errides all restriction." Perfection is ubiquity in space and possession of its contents, the "fresh variety" of the world which, in another poem from the same volume, leaves the poet "perplexed by detail." The celebrated slogan, "No ideas but in things," is a shorthand expression of the identification of mind and universe presupposed in Williams's work. Other people are no different from inanimate objects and may just as well incarnate the poet's ideas. This obliteration of distances also takes place in the relation between the poet and his readers. "In the imagination," he says, "we are from henceforth (so long as you read) locked in a fraternal embrace, the classic caress of author and reader. We are one. Whenever I say 'I' I mean also 'you'" [*Spring and All* (Dijon: Contact, 1923); all further references to this text will be abbreviated as *SA*]. To accept the embrace Williams offers means the impossibility of "criticizing" his work, if criticism means viewing with the cold eye of analysis and judgment. The critic must resign himself to the poet's world and accept what he finds there.

If the poetry of the last century and a half has often assumed a distance between man and things or between man and man, an equally important theme has been the distance of God. Here too Williams differs from his predecessors. In his work there is no searching for the traces of a vanished deity, no frantic attempt to find a new mediator between heaven and earth. "Heaven," he says in one of his few references to the idea of another world, "seems frankly impossible" [*SL*]. The disappearance of a distinction between subject and object could be said to mark the end of a tradition which began in its modern form with writers like Montaigne, Pascal, Descartes, and Locke, those explorers of the abyss of subjectivity. The absence of the idea of heaven means the rejection of an even older tradition, Christian and Platonic. Here is everywhere for Williams, and there is no other world to go to.

The resignation to existence which makes Williams's poetry possible is the exact reverse of the Cartesian Cogito. Descartes puts everything in question in order to establish the existence of his separate self, an existence built on the power of detached thinking. Williams gives himself up in despair and establishes a self beyond personality, a self coextensive with the universe. Words, things, people, and God vanish as separate entities and everything becomes a unit. In "The Wanderer" this obliteration of distinctions is poetically enacted. Under the aegis of a muse-lady (whom Williams has identified with his grandmother, the poet is absorbed into the Passaic, swallowed up by "the utter depth of its rottenness"

[*CEP*], or it can be said that he takes the river into himself, for it is an inter-penetration, both ways. After this plunge he possesses all time and space and has complete knowledge of everything: "I knew all—it became me" [*CEP*].

This phrase is quoted near the end of Book Five of *Paterson*, in a context which shows the poet's awareness of its seminal place in his work. After the absorption of the poet by the river the muse speaks once more to him: "Be mostly silent!" [*CEP*]. Here is attained that silence and anonymity which he describes in the letter to Marianne Moore. This silence is his marriage to all that is.

"Be mostly silent!" How can this be? In the years after "The Wanderer," Williams was anything but silent. He wrote poems, plays, stories, and essays in a constant stream. How can he have gone from his silence to a justification of literature?

Words as the expression of man's separation from things disappear with the poet's plunge into the Passaic, but this does not mean that language vanishes. It reappears in the new silence as something which already exists, like trees and rocks. Williams's poetry takes language for granted, just as it takes chicory, daisies, plums, and butterfish for granted. His plunge into the substance of things does not reach a shapeless blur in which all distinctions have been lost. The world is within rather than at a distance, but it is still full of things existing in the exactness of their forms. Beside the other things are words. Language has a kind of sanctity for Williams, and most of his vocabulary can be found in any pocket dictionary. There is scarcely a trace in his poetry of that attempt to recon-struct language by deformation which characterizes a writer like Joyce.

Words are first of all things: "But can you not see, can you not taste, can you not smell, can you not hear, can you not touch—words? . . . Words roll, spin, flare up, rumble, trickle, foam—" [*GAN*]. A word is its sound and feel in the mouth when spoken, or the way it looks on the page, black marks against a white background, graphite which could be "scraped up and put in a tube" or ink which could be lifted from the page [*GAN*]. As a painting is made of paint or music of sound, so "A poem is a small (or large) machine made of words" [*SE*]. This does not mean that Williams wants to drain words of meaning and make them dull surds, mute lumps of voiceless matter. "Words are indivisible crystals," and if they are broken up nothing is left but meaningless letters: "Awu tsst grang splith gra pragh og bm" [*GAN*]. To suppose that words in themselves are meaningless would be a return to one form of the dualism Williams has escaped. In the realm where man and things are one there is nothing which is not intrinsically meaningful. To suppose that man ascribes meaning to things is to suppose a separation of subject and object. Every gesture, every flower, every stone has its meaning as part of its substance, and words contain their meaning as an inextricable part of themselves. Like gestures or facial expressions they are ways man affirms his solidarity with the world, proof that meaning is always incarnated, never purely spiritual. "The words," says the poet, "must become real, they must take the place of wife and sweetheart. They must be a church— Wife. It must be your wife. It must be a thing of adamant with the texture of wind. Wife" [GAN]. In another sentence the attempt to make words substantial expressed in the repetitions here of "wife" is affirmed as successful: "The words from long practice had come to be leaves, trees, the corners of his house" [GAN].

This acceptance of words as things manifests itself in several ways in Williams's work. Sometimes words are taken as *objets trouvés*. A modern painter makes his collage of bits of newspaper or cigarette packages. Picasso creates a bull's head out of a bicycle seat and handle bars. Marcel Duchamp sets up a urinal as a "ready-made." In the same way Williams makes poetry out of a list of kinds of ice cream, with prices [CEP], or out of street signs [CEP], or out of a fashionable grocery list: "2 partridges / 2 mallard ducks / a Dungeness crab / 24 hours out / of the Pacific / and 2 live-frozen / trout / from Denmark" [P]. Nonverbal things cannot be put into poetry, since poems are after all made of words, but words also are ready-made and may be taken out of their contexts and put into a poem just as they are found. It is not necessary to change something to make it poetic. All things, including words, are already poetic, and what the painter does with bits of burlap and old nails the poet may do with words, put them without arrangement on the page, so they will be present—*there*.

Williams uses in this way quotations from history books, interviews, and letters. The prose parts of *Paterson* are not "antipoetry" set against the poetry of the parts in verse. The prose is poetry too, and the insertion of big chunks of unshaped language as it was spontaneously used is another way of showing that all language is intrinsically poetic. "All the prose," says the poet of *Paterson*, ". . . has primarily the purpose of giving a metrical meaning to or of emphasizing a metrical continuity between all word use. It is *not* an antipoetic device, the repeating of which piece of miscalculation makes me want to puke. It *is* that prose and verse are both *writing*, both a matter of the words and an interrelation between words for the purpose of exposition, or other better defined purpose of the art. . . . The truth is that there's an *identity* between prose and verse, not an antithesis. It all rests on the same time base, the same measure" [SL]. The sonnet form or iambic pentameter are preconceived molds, imported from another continent. To force American material into these foreign shapes is to falsify them. Our speech has new rhythms and a new structure: "We've got to *begin* by stating that we speak (here) a distinct, separate language in a present (new era) and that it is NOT English" [SL]. The poet's job is to find examples of the American measure, newborn in all their purity, and put them in his poems for all to hear.

The prose of *Paterson* is made of language the poet found already written down. The language in his stories, in his book about his mother, and in some of

his poems is living speech, snatches of conversation or soliloquy which he over-
heard, recorded, and preserved. Many of the stories consist almost entirely of
such "auditory scraps from the language" [SL]. They have no plot, no dramatic
climax. Their virtue is to catch the language as it was spoken. A doctor has
unique chances to know at first hand the poetic vitality of the common language,
and much of Williams's fiction derives from his medical experience. "It is then
we see," he says, "by this constant feeling for a meaning, from the unselected
nature of the material, just as it comes in over the phone or at the office door,
that there is no better way to get an intimation of what is going on in the world.
. . . The physician enjoys a wonderful opportunity actually to witness the words
being born. Their actual colors and shapes are laid before him carrying their tiny
burdens which he is privileged to take into his care with their unspoiled newness"
[Autobiography].

Speech is an attribute of its speaker, part of what he does or is in the same
way that a rose is red or a bit of glass green and shiny. Here again Williams
rejects any attempt to make words "spiritual," inhabitants of a detached world
of consciousness. A woman's smile, her walk, a child's way of bouncing a ball —
these are manifestations of the substance of a person, aspects of the world's body
brought to light. Words are gestures too, an uncovering of hidden life. Yes, Mrs.
Williams is made up largely of the record of things the poet heard his mother
say. The disconnected scraps of Mrs. Williams's speech are not an imaginative
"portrait." They are the woman herself made visible, each phrase "bringing all
together to return the world to simplicity again," showing her as "a valuable
thing," "something to look at and to know with satisfaction, something alive."
In the same way the poems often record with relish the common idiom just as it
was spoken:

> Doc, I bin lookin' for you
> I owe you two bucks.
> [CEP]

> . . . Geeze, Doc, I guess it's all right
> but what the hell does it mean?
> [P]

To show words as things containing their meaning it is sometimes enough
to record the visible words of street signs and menus, the audible words of common speech, but language can get encrusted with old emotions and ideological
associations. When this happens its validity is lost. The people of Paterson cannot communicate with one another or with the ground which ought to support
them: "The language, the language / fails them." Authentic language springs

from the present moment. Words pasted over with past associations make up part of that film which hangs between man and reality. "There is a constant barrier between the reader and his consciousness of immediate contact with the world. . . . [N]early all writing, up to the present, if not all art, has been especially designed to keep up the barrier between sense and the vaporous fringe which distracts the attention from its agonized approaches to the moment" [SA]. Against this traditional commitment to an art of "the beautiful illusion" Williams sets his art of immediacy. "We have no words. Every word we get must be broken off from the European mass. Every word we get placed over again by some delicate hand. Piece by piece we must loosen what we want" [GAN]. There must be a "cracking up of phrases which have stopped the mind." The end of such an appropriation and renewal of language is "to refine, to clarify, to intensify that eternal moment in which we alone live" [SA]. This can take place only through a cleansing of words, so that they stand upright on the page, naked and immediate, separate from all previous uses of them, separate even from one another. Marianne Moore uses words in this way, and Williams's praise of her way with words is a covert description of his own aim: "Miss Moore gets great pleasure from wiping soiled words or cutting them clean out, removing the aureoles that have been pasted about them or taking them bodily from greasy contexts. For the compositions which Miss Moore intends, each word should first stand crystal clear with no attachments; not even an aroma" [SE].

How can a word be renewed in this way, "separated out by science, treated with acid to remove the smudges, washed, dried and placed right side up on a clean surface" [SE], with all its primitive strength intact, a thing embodying its meaning? It can be done partly by a chastity in the choice of words. Simple words predominate in Williams's poetry, those words all men must use, so that they always live freshly in the present, reborn of its need. Vocabulary, however, is not enough. A word in itself has no meaning, but is a power of combining with other words. Meaning emerges from the structural relations of a group of words together. Since this is so the naked virtue of a word is often invisible in a sentence. Each word melts into its context and vanishes as a thing in itself, but Williams's aim is precisely to make the word visible as a thing in itself. To allow a word to be absorbed by the language surrounding it is as bad as to let it be swallowed up in its traditional associations. The poet's words must "remain separate, each unwilling to group with the others except as they move in the one direction" [SA]. To put down a single word in the middle of a blank sheet of paper achieves nothing but the flatness of a dictionary. Each word must be set against others, for only then does it take on force and reality, but at the same time it must be used "in such a way that it will remain scrupulously itself, clean perfect, unnicked beside other words in parade" [SE].

A manipulation of syntax is one way to reach this difficult goal. The poet must return to the primitive elements of language if a new measure is to be created. The sentence must be pulverized and recreated from the ground up. This does not mean wild, disordered, or novel grammar. It means isolating the fundamental ways words combine, concern for the way words grapple with one another to form meanings. This syntactical energy is concentrated on in itself. Gertrude Stein is praised by Williams not only for her "emphasis on the word as object," but for her investigations into the "grammatical play" of words, her power to reveal "the skeleton, the 'formal' parts of writing, those that make form" [SE]. In Williams's own poetry such an attention to syntax is everywhere evident, a focus on what Gerard Manley Hopkins called "the naked thew and sinew" of the language. Words are grouped in brief simple phrases which combine with other phrases to form the grammar of the whole:

> My shoes as I lean
> unlacing them
> stand out upon
> flat worsted flowers.
>
> Nimbly the shadows
> of my fingers play
> unlacing
> over shoes and flowers.
>   [CEP]

The simplicity of the sentence structure here, and the emphasis on the tensions between the words makes them stand separate and yet together. Rhythm also works to achieve this end. Williams's metrical effects have an extraordinary power to bring each word out in its "thingness," to make the reader pause over it and savor its tang before going on to the next word. Like the bushes, small trees, and weeds in "By the road to the contagious hospital," each word stands on its own, though sprung from the same ground as the others. The independence of the words in the poem matches the independence of the things they name. The short lines and brief monosyllables of Williams's verse have exactly the opposite effect from the long rapidly rolling blurred periods of Whitman's line, with its tendency to absorb all particulars into one sonorous whole. In the stately slowness of Williams's cadence things and words retain their integrity:

> All along the road the reddish
> purplish, forked, upstanding, twiggy
> stuff of bushes and small trees
> with dead, brown leaves under them
> leafless vines —
>   [CEP]

The poet's characteristic rhythm separates words from one another, or combines several, gently but firmly, into a unit which does not obliterate the outlines of even the most insignificant word. In his verse, as in the growth of things in spring, "One by one objects are defined— / It quickens: clarity, outline of leaf" [*CEP*]. This effect is supported by his way of breaking up his lines. A poem is "a thing made up of words and punctuation, that is, words and the spaces between them" ["An Approach to the Poem," *English Institute Essays: 1947* (New York: Columbia University Press, 1948)]. Just as a modern sculptor shapes space with stone and makes it visible, so Williams's poems bring into the open the white flatness of the page on which the words are printed—not, however, as a "nothingness," the virgin whiteness which the blank spaces in Mallarmé's poems defend. Williams's spaces are full of tension and life, and in them shines that goal toward which the words all singly move. A beautiful early poem, in which rain is the living substance of love, makes this explicit:

> So my life is spent
> > to keep out love
> with which
> she rains upon
>
> > the world
>
> of spring
>
> > drips
>
> so spreads
>
> > the words
>
> far apart to let in
>
> > her love
> > [*CEP*]

A pregnant tension is given to words and the spaces around them by ending a line in the middle of a phrase. Partly this is done to affirm that the sound and weight of a word, in its relation to those around it, is more important than its grammatical connections. Words are treated as things grouped together to form metrical feet, and it is too bad for the grammar if a foot happens to end in the middle of a phrase. The effect of breaking the line in this way is quite different from the isolation of a word in the dictionary. The word at the end of a line may be an adjective without a noun, or a preposition with no phrase to complete it, or a conjunction hanging in the air, as in the following complete lines:

of red and

be a song—made of

mottled clouds driven from the

It is too old, the

splash of a half purple, half

but

flash a

of the

In such lines each word, especially the last, stands alone, with its full vocative or ejaculatory emphasis, but the reader knows that the last word is part of a grammatical construction and will be completed in the next line. The word is not by itself, in slackness, but is endowed with its power of connecting itself to other words in a network of meaning. The word reaches out with all its strength toward the other words which are for the moment absent. Conjunctions, prepositions, adjectives, when they come at the end of a line, assume an expressive energy as arrows of force reaching toward the other words: "of red and →." Going for the moment toward the void, they go all the more strongly, as a man in isolation reaches out in longing toward other men and women. Into the white space surrounding the word go a multitude of lines of force, charging that space with the almost tangible presence of the various words which might come to complete the central word and appease its tension.

The poem called "The Yellow Chimney" demonstrates the way this technique can make words take on substance and presence. A series of lines end in color-words which are completed with nouns at the beginning of the next lines: "fleshpale/smoke," "blue/sky," "silver/rings," "yellow/brick." This sets up a pattern so that further lines can achieve the same effect by ending with ordinarily insignificant words, mere connectives, prepositions, articles, conjunctions, "that," "at," "not," "of," "but," "the." The poem gives these words too their proper weight and reality. This power to make the reader see that such words are as much things as are nouns and verbs is one of the supreme triumphs of Williams's art:

There is a plume
of fleshpale
smoke upon the blue

sky. The silver
rings that
strap the yellow

brick stack at
wide intervals shine
in this amber

light—not
of the sun not of
the pale sun but

his born brother
the
declining season
                    [*The Collected Later Poems*]

Rhythm, syntax, and the placing of the words operate here, as again and
again in Williams's poetry, to achieve, through "the design of [the] sentences"
[*SE*], that isolation of words from their logical or abstract meaning for which the
poet praises Laurence Sterne and Gertrude Stein: "The feeling is of words themselves, a curious immediate quality quite apart from their meaning, much as in
music different notes are dropped, so to speak, into repeated chords one at a
time, one after the other—for themselves alone" [*SE*]. Better than the temporal
metaphor of music might be a spatial metaphor, like that of "primitive masonry,
the units unglued and as in the greatest early constructions unstandardized" [*SE*],
on which Williams models his prose in "The Destruction of Tenochtitlan." The
result of his dissociation of words from one another, from their past associations,
and from their "dead weight of logical burdens" [*SE*] is the achievement of that
spatiality which Gaston Bachelard and others see as one tendency of modern art.
Williams wants his poems to have movement and praises that quality in poetic
language. A poet's words should:

            bite
                their way
        home—being actual

        having the form
                of motion
                    [*CEP*]

The immediacy necessary for authentic language, however, means that the
movement of a poem must be confined to the moment. Even his longest poems,

Williams: Poet of Reality

Paterson, *The Desert Music*, or *Asphodel, That Greeny Flower*, produce an effect of simultaneity. In them many actions are going on at once in a perpetual present, the poetic space, and though the images are necessarily sequential they form a chord which exists in a single moment. His shorter poems, though full of movement, are even more obviously spatial. Their motion takes place in one instant, before the reader, on the page, so that a poem like "The Yellow Chimney" is a picture of what it represents, the slender column of words corresponding to the chimney, and the lines of the poem, it may not be too fanciful to say, echoing the silver rings which strap the yellow stack at intervals. Other poems where this form of correspondence cannot be seen are no less spatial. The words are like shapes in a mosaic, all pulling and pushing against one another at once. This spatialization, as well as the tension between words and the page behind them, is expressed in a metaphor from Williams's essay on Marianne Moore. Her words, like his, are "white circular discs grouped closely edge to edge upon a dark table [which] make black six-pointed stars" [*SE*].

Words treated in this way become interjections, exclamatory vocables, substances of sound divorced from any abstract meaning and returned to their primitive power as explosions of linguistic energy, each with its own precise radiance. The relations between the words seem less those of grammatical meaning than the attractions caused by the juxtaposition of energies. In this pulverization of language words become atomic particles moving violently like the little wavelets in one of Williams's important motifs—a volume filled with a multiplicity of wriggling forces—waves, worms, stars, yachts contending in the sea.

The poet not unexpectedly endorses Charles Olson's theory of "composition by field" [*Autobiography*]. "The poem is made of things—on a field," and therefore is an example of what Marshall McLuhan calls "a mode of broken or syncopated manipulation to permit *inclusive* or simultaneous perception of a total and diversified field." Williams frequently recognizes the way each of his poems is a dynamic motion within a field of forces, as when he says: "You must know by this time that my liking is for an unimpeded thrust right through a poem from the beginning to the end, without regard to formal arrangements" [*SL*]. In the "Prologue to *Kora in Hell*" he defines the poetic space as a moving field which the poet opposes to achieve tension: "The stream of things having composed itself into wiry strands that move in one fixed direction, the poet in desperation turns at right angles and cuts across current with startling results to his hangdog mood" [*SE*]. In another text: "the words must be recognized to be moving in a direction separate from the jostling or lack of it which occurs within the piece" [*SA*]. A sentence "undulates," or the space of a poem is defined as "one / jittering direction made of all / directions spelling the inexplicable" [*The Collected Later Poems* (New York: New Directions, 1963); all further references to this text will be abbreviated as *CLP*]. This space is usually characterized by dissonance rather than by smooth harmony, as Williams affirms when he defends, in an interview with Mike Wallace, the passage in his poetry about two partridges, two mallard ducks, a Dungeness crab: "—if you treat that rhythmically, ignoring the practical sense, it forms a jagged pattern" [*P*].

Within the field of the poem there must be, as in Stevens's early poetry, a tense equilibrium of opposed energies. Otherwise the words will go toward one pole, gather there, and the poem will disappear along with the field which constituted it. The poem must be "balanced between / eternities" [*P*]. *Kora in Hell* is a sequence of free variations on this theme of polarity. The motif dominant in the prose poems is defended in the commentaries on them: "Between two contending forces there may at all times arrive that moment when the stress is equal on both sides so that with a great pushing a great stability results giving a picture of perfect rest"; "Often when the descent seems well marked there will be a subtle ascent over-ruling it so that in the end when the degradation is fully anticipated the person will be found to have emerged upon a hilltop." Even in Williams's latest work a whole poem or passage in a poem is often made up of the interaction of a group of ascending or descending energies. Such poems achieve that "rout of the vocables" which the poet praises in Gertrude Stein [*P*]. The words and phrases are like those birds and leaves in Book Five of *Paterson*: "All together, working together— / all the birds together. The birds / and leaves are designed to be woven / in his mind eating and   . . / all together for his purposes." Language creates an inner space of polarized energies, and this space, with all its contents, moves as a unit toward its goal.

"The Locust Tree in Flower" or *Paterson* or the poems in *Pictures from Brueghel* establish a place of simultaneity. "The mind's a queer sponge / squeeze it and out come bird songs / small leaves highly enameled / and . moments of good reading" [*CLP*]. Within the sponge mind each thing touches the others, interacting with them, quarreling, rebounding, and yet keeping its definite edges and form. Each fills space, permeates it, but remains itself, uncontaminated by the others, and each is at once substantial, mental, and linguistic. To read *Paterson* or *Asphodel, That Greeny Flower* is to enter a region where everything the poet has ever experienced is present together, each item in its particularity ready to be called on when it is needed. This kind of space is expressed by the basic metaphor of *Paterson*: the Passaic River with its falls. The water is the ground of mind, of things, and of language; its roar contains them all. In *Paterson* the plunge into the Passaic which the poet had made in "The Wanderer" is explored in its deepest implications, and flowing water is established as the fundamental metaphor of the new realm Williams's poetry creates:

> Jostled as are the waters approaching
> the brink, his thoughts
> interlace, repel and cut under,
> rise rock-thwarted and turn aside
> but forever strain forward.

Words as things incarnating their meanings become a set of fluid energies whose life exists only in the present. Such words, isolated and cleaned, can be put down on the page like splashes of paint on a canvas and allowed to explode into the multitude of meanings which emerge from their juxtaposition. One version of "The Locust Tree in Flower" is an extreme example of this use of words. Here each word has a line to itself, and is surrounded on all sides by the blank page. Logic and grammar almost disappear, but not quite, and prepositions, adjectives, nouns, verbs, and adverbs are put side by side to establish a simultaneous pattern of linguistic forces. This effect is enhanced by the fact that the poem begins with two prepositions, which must be held side by side in the mind as alternatives. Then follow a series of somewhat contradictory adjectives without the article which would be expected before a singular noun. Are these all meant to modify "branch," or will a later noun attract some of them to itself? The words hang freely in the air. Moreover, the verb presupposes a plural subject, so the reader must balance between the possibility that the word "has" may have been left out and the assumption that "come" is to be taken as an imperative. This grammatical uncertainty forces him to hold all the words before his attention at once as he tries various ways to make a sentence of them. He is like a seal juggling thirteen brightly colored balls, and this is exactly what the poet wants. The poem is as much all there at once as the locust tree itself, in its tension of branches, leaves, and flowers. The poem is not a picture of the tree, but is itself something substantial echoing in its structure of verbal forces the birth of white blossoms from stiff boughs. In "The Locust Tree in Flower," to borrow Williams's praise for Miss Moore, the "purely stated idea," the idea embodied in words which are things, "has an edge exactly like a fruit or a tree or a serpent" [*SE*]:

> Among
> of
> green
>
> stiff
> old
> bright

broken
branch
come

white
sweet
May

again

Words, nevertheless, are different from splashes of paint or musical sounds. However consubstantial their meaning and their physical presence, they still refer to things other than themselves. The word "parsley" is the name of a small green crinkly plant. Williams cannot escape the referential meaning of words, and curiously enough he has none of that tormenting fear of reference which haunts modern art, no desire to abolish the naming power of words in order to create a poem which will be entirely free of objects, like an abstract painting. In his poetry words are one thing, trees and flowers are another, but both are possessed within the same inner space. As a result he replaces the romantic or symbolist aesthetic of transformation with an art which is calm description, naming one by one the visible and tangible qualities of an object. Texts of this sort abound in his work:

In brilliant gas light
I turn the kitchen spigot
and watch the water plash
into the clean white sink.

On the grooved drain-board
to one side is
a glass filled with parsley—
crisped green.

[CEP]

Such a passage is the exact opposite of a poetry of indirection or of transposition, Mallarmé's hints at the fan which he never names or Stevens's tangents of a pineapple. Williams can look straight at the object because it offers no threat. There is nothing alien or distant about it. It proposes no invitation to the poet's violence. The objectivity of his descriptions affirms his security. The parsley does not need the poem. The poem does not need the parsley. The parsley and the poem about the parsley are separate things, each existing within the universal realm made of the poet's coextension with the world. Poetry of this kind is a way of letting things be. A good poet, consequently, "doesn't *select* his material. What is there to select? It *is*."

To let the parsley be in the poem does not mean transposing the parsley into the poem. It means using the referential meaning of words to name the parsley in its self-sustaining independence. The parsley is a stubborn and irreducible fact, nonverbal in nature, and the poem in the simplicity of its description recognizes it as such. Just as the parsley is separate from the poem about it, so it is separate from the things around it. It stands alone in its glass, side by side with the grooved drainboard, the clean white sink, the water, the spigot, the gaslight. Each thing has its own intrinsic particularity, its own precise edges cutting it off from other things, just as each word in "The Locust Tree in Flower" stands by itself, surrounded by the white page. There is no blurring, no flowing of a ubiquitous force which melts distinctions and makes things alike. In the "Prologue to *Kora in Hell*" the poet affirms that the value of his poem about the chicory flower (see *CEP*) is the way it praises the resolute isolation of the plant. Free of the poem, it is also free of the things around it: "A poet witnessing the chicory flower and realizing its virtues of form and color so constructs his praise of it as to borrow no particle from right or left. He gives his poem over to the flower and its plant themselves" [*SE*]. In Williams's world there are no resonances or similarities between things, no basis for metaphor. There is in fact little figurative language in his poetry. He is deeply suspicious of it. Its place is sometimes taken by a version of imagist technique, the juxtaposition of dissonant things so that a meaning may emerge from their contrast:

> Like a cylindrical tank fresh silvered
> upended on the sidewalk to advertise
> some plumber's shop, a profusion
> of pink roses bending ragged in the rain—
>
> [*CLP*]

Most often even this doubling of particulars is not permitted. Williams has an extraordinary ability to pick a single thing out of the multitude existing and focus on it with intense concentration, as if it were the only object in the world, incomparable, unique. He has the power of "seeing the thing itself without forethought or afterthought but with great intensity of perception" which he praises in his mother [*SE*]. His attitude toward things, like Ezra Pound's, is nominalist. Each object is itself and nothing more should be said about it: "Although it is a quality of the imagination that it seeks to place together those things which have a common relationship, yet the coining of similes is a pastime of very low order, depending as it does upon a nearly vegetable coincidence. Much more keen is that power which discovers in things those inimitable particles of dissimilarity to all other things which are the peculiar perfections of the thing in question."

Nor are there vertical resonances. Since there is no "behind" or "beyond" in Williams's world, no depth or transcendence, there can be no symbolic meaning in things, no reference to a secret heaven of ideal values. "No symbolism is acceptable" [SE]; "Those who permit their senses to be despoiled of the things under their noses by stories of all manner of things removed and unattainable are of frail imagination." A primrose is just a primrose, and there are no deep thoughts in flowers, trees, or tables. The table "describes / nothing: four legs, by which / it becomes a table" [CLP]. The wheelbarrow, in a famous poem, does not stand for anything or mean anything. It is an object in space dissociated from the objects around it, without reference beyond itself. It is what it is. The aim of the poem is to make it stand there for the reader in its separateness, as the words of the poem stand on the page.

If the poem affirms the independence of the object and lets the object be, what good is the poem in itself? The parsley already is, and there seems little use for a poem which merely says that it is. Williams's response to this problem is the basis of his theory of imagination. The poet must make use of the referential meaning of words to relate them to physical objects as a springboard from which they may leap into a realm of imagination carrying with them the things named in a new form. Williams rejects those modern poets who "use unoriented sounds in place of conventional words" [SA]. Words should not be wholly independent of things, but they should not be completely attached to things either. That would be the kind of description in which "words adhere to certain objects, and have the effect on the sense of oysters, or barnacles." Poetry is an effect of the imagination, and "words occur in liberation by virtue of its processes." How can this freedom be attained? It is not a matter of "a removal from reality." There must be no return to the idea of the imagination as a power which can take the reader beyond the world. The imagination is one of the conditions or regions of the inner-outer space which is all there is. In poetry words must still have their old meanings, and, therefore, "the writer of imagination would attain closest to the conditions of music not when his words are disassociated from natural objects and specified meanings but when they are liberated from the usual quality of that meaning by transposition into another medium, the imagination."

This liberation takes place by a paradoxical movement both toward and away from the object, a movement of which the poem about parsley is an example. By illuminating the object exactly, the poem affirms the object's independence and thereby frees the words to execute their dance of imagination above the body of the world. The words carry with them some of the substance of the world and are vitalized by their possession of that substance. The thing "needs no personal support but exists free from human action," and the poem is real too, but only because it is both related to and free from the thing it names. "The word is not liberated," says Williams, "therefore able to communicate release from the fixities which destroy it until it is accurately tuned to the fact which giving it reality, by its own reality establishes its own freedom from the necessity of a word, thus freeing it and dynamizing it at the same time." This crucial passage explains what the poet means earlier when he says that "the same things exist, but in a different condition when energized by the imagination." An image of sublimation is fundamental to his concept of the action of imagination. Poetry lifts things up. Its aim is "to repair, to rescue, to complete" [SL]. John of Gaunt's speech in *Richard II*, for example, is not an escape from reality, nor is it a mere description of his state. It is "a dance over the body of his condition accurately accompanying it" [SA]. This idea of a free play of words above reality but not separate from it appears again in an image of poetry as like a bird in flight: "As birds' wings beat the solid air without which none could fly so words freed by the imagination affirm reality by their flight." In another passage, "the poet, challenging the event, recreates it as of whence it sprang from among men and women, and makes a new world of it."

This tense interaction between words and things is the basis of Williams's repeated affirmation that a poem is "a field of action" [SE]. Only if the words are both free of things and related to them can it be said that "poetry does not tamper with the world but moves it" [SA]. This avoids both the Scylla of defining art as a mirror of reality and the Charybdis of accepting an art of romantic evasion, a music of pure sounds cut off from life. The poem and the thing are both real, both equally real:

> A rose *is* a rose
> > and the poem equals it
> if it be well made.

Again and again the poet repeats his rejection of any representational theory of art. Poetry is "not a matter of 'representation' " [SA], "nor is it description nor an evocation of objects or situations." A poem "creates a new object, a play, a dance which is not a mirror up to nature," "not 'like' anything but transfused with the same forces which transfuse the earth—at least one small part of them." The prose parts of the original edition of *Spring and All*, never reprinted by the poet, are his fullest expressions of a subtle theory of poetry which rejects both the mirror and the lamp, both the classical theory of art as imitation, and the romantic theory of art as transformation. In their place is proposed a new objectivist art in which a poem is "Not prophecy! NOT prophecy! / but the thing itself!" [P]. This new art is becoming increasingly dominant in both America and Europe, and, as this happens, Williams's place as a poet helping to bring about a radical change in literature is more apparent.

If the same energies flow through a poem as flow through the earth, then a poem is "natural" because it is a growth, a process. The poet must try to write "the poem that lifts the dish / of fruit . . . like / a table" [CLP], or compose fiction "so that when [he speaks] of a chair it will stand upon four legs in a room. And of course it will stand upon a four-legged sentence on a page at the same time" [SL]. These passages emphasize the activity of the poem. The poem "lifts" the dish of fruit, or "stands up" on the page. Elsewhere the way the essence of poetry is its power to do something is even more explicit. Only if the poem shifts from the adjective which copies a dead nature to the verb which is alive with natural forces can the words be an extension of the processes of the earth, "not 'realism' but reality itself" [SA]:

> To copy nature is a spineless activity; it gives us a sense of our mere existence but hardly more than that. But to imitate nature involves the verb: we then ourselves become nature, and so invent an object which is an extension of the process.
>
> [SL]

> It is not to place adjectives, it is to learn to employ the verbs in imitation of nature—so that the pieces move naturally—and watch, often breathlessly, what they *do*.
>
> [SE]

"Only the made poem, the verb calls it / into being." The verbal energy of the poem makes it part of nature and asserts the poet's approximate coextension with the universe. Williams ridicules the idea that this means some impossible Roman feast in which man ingurgitates the earth: "the powers of a man are so pitifully small, with the ocean to swallow—that at the end of the feast nothing would be left but suicide" [SA]. Through the action of imagination the poet frees himself from this absurd thirst or hunger. When he has rooted himself in objective reality his poems become "as actual, as sappy as the leaf of the tree which never moves from one spot." His coextension with the universe need be only approximate, for the sap in his poems flows everywhere. This sharing in universal energies produces the sense of "enlargement," of "expansion," which men feel "before great or good work."

The need to have the poem rooted in the ground of reality is the reason for Williams's insistence that art must start with the local and particular, and raise those to the universal. The poet is "taught by the largeness of his imagination to feel every form which he sees moving within himself" [SA]. His problem is "to be both local (all art is local) and at the same time to surmount that restriction by climbing to the universal in all art" [SL]. By concentrating on the individual in its uniqueness the poet may reach the universal. The particular *is* the universal. The same forces stream through it as stream through all existence, and therefore the poet "seems to make the world come toward him to brush against the spines of his shrub. So that in looking at some apparently small object one feels the swirl of great events" [SE]. It is for this reason that so much depends upon the red wheelbarrow. The wheelbarrow, red and glazed with rain water, occupying silently its small spot in time and space, contains everything. In the same way a single word may concentrate the poet and his world in a breath, as the poet somewhat whimsically proposes in *The Great American Novel*: "I shall make myself into a word. One big word. One big union. . . . I begin small and make myself into a big splurging word: I take life and make it into one big blurb." Whatever the specific content of the here and now may be, it can still be said that "all things enter into the singleness of the moment and the moment partakes of the diversity of all things" [SE]. The poems about chicory and parsley, like the chicory and parsley themselves, concentrate in themselves the universe, and the basic method of art is that recommended at the beginning of *Paterson*:

> To make a start,
> out of particulars
> and make them general.

. . . Apparently there is no farther to go with Williams. Anywhere is everywhere, and there are no directions, nothing to do, nowhere to move after a first moment which contains everything, the senses having taken all objects into a realm where things are ideas, ideas things. The problems which gave rise to action in earlier literature have disappeared: no difficulty in knowing other people; no uncertain approach to external objects by the subjective mind; no pathos of a distant and unattainable God. Poetry in such a world seems to be limited to variations on a first instant which contains everything and appeases every desire.

There is, however, much drama in Williams's work, but it lies in a dimension appropriate to the realm of immanence which he has entered. Three elements are always present in that realm, and these must be brought into the proper relation or life will fall back to some form of inauthenticity. Yet they are mutually incompatible. When one is present the others tend to disappear or to be occulted. Like matter and anti-matter they destroy one another. Only with great difficulty can they be brought into balance. All Williams's work is an attempt to discover ways to do this.

The three elements are the formless ground, origin of all things; the formed thing, defined and limited; a nameless presence, the "beautiful thing" [P], there in every form but hidden by it. The ground is what is always already there, chaotic, senseless, absurd, but fecund, holding within itself the possibility of all forms. The "unfathomable ground / where we walk daily" [*CLP*] is perpetually new, untouched by time, because it is always in its original state, unshaped, un-fixed, a "muddy flux" [*P*] with an inexhaustible energy of being.

This elemental substance appears throughout Williams's work as the genera-tive source. It is the Passaic, in "The Wanderer," in which the poet is plunged to lose his separate identity. It is the earth, in "Sub Terra," the first poem in *Al Que Quiere!* It is "the earth under our feet" in "At Kenneth Burke's Place." It is present in poem after poem as that which any form has risen from, or stands upon, or is seen against, the common earth, "the clay of these parts" [*CEP*] which exerts its drag toward formlessness on the poet, as the sea in "The Yachts" tries to pull down the graceful boats. The ground may be common to all men at all times, but the Europeans coming to America found that "the ground [had] undergone / a subtle transformation, its identity altered" [*P*]. *In the American Grain* is Williams's chronicle of the settlers' response to the unfamiliar texture of an alien ground. It tells of their obliteration of the cultures which had flowered naturally there, the culture of the North American Indians, the culture of Tenoch-titlán, a "whole world of . . . unique associations" which Cortéz destroyed, so that it "sank back into the ground to be reënkindled, never." The ground is also present in multiple disguises throughout *Paterson*, where the poet has "a mass of detail / to interrelate on a new ground, difficultly." It is the earth itself, present in one passage as a tabular account of the forms of rock in layers down to 2100 feet in a well at Paterson. It is the river and its falls, shapeless, fluid, an inarticu-late roar. It is the fire of Book Three, "a cataract reversed, shooting / upward." It is the wind in the same book, and the "alluvial silt" left after a flood, "a sort of muck, a detritus, / in this case—a pustular scum, a decay, a choking / life-lessness." Earth, "cyclone, fire / and flood"—the unfathomable ground is present in all the elements. Out of these four everything has sprung.

The ground is the source of more than the flowers, trees, and bushes which grip down their roots and thrust toward the sky in so many of Williams's poems. Earth, the chatterer, is also father of speech. Words spring from the ground and each is another form of the primitive word spoken by the falls in its roaring, like the "Blouaugh!" of the sea-elephant, which is the speech of the deep sea [*CEP*]. Each human being, mind incarnate in a body, has also come from the earth. In "The Cure" the poet tells his lady of that ground "from which / among the rest you have sprung / and opened flower-like to my hand." Words, things, people— all three have the same origin, and this guarantees their harmonious copresence in the poem. Language, objects, and minds have the same father, and "like father, like son," so the words of the poem can be the place where ideas are things. The new measure Williams seeks, with its dance of the vocables, is another mode of the rising of shape from the unfathomable ground.

Though earth is origin of all form the two are radically opposed, as shape is opposed to shapeless, measure to the measureless, the limited to the illimitable. To have one seems to mean the loss of the other. The chthonic vitality of the moist earth is imperceptible in the airy fragility of the flower, and the flower cut off from the earth is dead, like that symbol of separation and inauthenticity in *Paterson*: "a bud forever green, / tight-curled, upon the pavement, perfect / in juice and substance but divorced, divorced / from its fellows, fallen low—." Any form which is disjoined from the living earth is without value. An example of this is the academic mind, dry and abstract, imposing its dead forms on life. T. S. Eliot represents aridity of this sort in poetry, a return to European ideas and poetic forms, an attempt to perpetuate the past, ignoring the novel vitality of the present. "The past is for those who / lived in the past," and those who reverse this law are contributing to that divorce which is "the sign of knowledge in our time."

Williams's animus against the Puritans has the same source. Instead of opening themselves to the new land of America and creating a unique culture resting "upon peculiar and discoverable ground" [*In the American Grain* (New York: New Directions, 1956); all further references to this text will be abbreviated as *IAG*], they constructed in a vacuum a false culture modeled abstractly on the old European one:

> They must have closed all the world out. It was the enormity of their task that enforced it. Having in themselves nothing of curiosity, no wonder, for the New World—that is nothing official—they knew only to keep their eyes blinded, their tongues in orderly manner between their teeth, their ears stopped by the monotony of their hymns and their flesh covered in straight habits. . . . It is an immorality that IS America. Here it began. You see the cause. There was no ground to build on, with a ground all blossoming about them—under their noses.

The citizens of Paterson have inherited the immorality on which America was founded. They too are surrounded with the opaque walls of a false culture. Their detachment from reality is especially apparent in the inauthenticity of their language: "They do not know the words / or have not / the courage to use them   ." It does not matter whether an abstract form is imported from the outside, or whether an indigenous form is allowed to become divorced from its roots. Whenever a linguistic, physical, or human form is separated from the parent ground it dies. For Williams, as for Stevens, reality lies only in the present moment, and any form must continue to draw its energy from the living earth. Everything must constantly be made anew through reimmersion in the originating

soil. Williams's fierce antipathy to all traditionalisms originates in these assump-
tions. "Root, Branch & Flower" —this was to be the title of his autobiography.
The phrase states concisely a basic pattern of his thought.

If the green bud divorced from branch and root dies, it is possible to sink
so deeply in the soil that all limitation is lost, and with it the power to flower
in a new shape. The city-dwellers of Paterson, divorced from a rooted culture,
are like flowers unfertilized by any bee. They return unfulfilled to the formless
source:

> They sink back into the loam
>   crying out
> —you may call it a cry
> that creeps over them, a shiver
>   as they wilt and disappear

In the American Grain celebrates those backwoodsmen, Boone, Houston,
and the rest, who "made contact with the intrinsic elements of an as yet un-
realized material of which the country was made" [*SE*]. The price for this contact
was extreme. They were gradually absorbed by the indistinctions of the wilderness, just as earlier De Soto was lured to his death by the land. The frontiersmen
could not return and achieve the triumph of a new form: "Such men had no way
of making their realizations vocal. They themselves became part of the antago-
nistic wilderness against which the coastal settlements were battling. Their sadness alone survives. Many of them could hardly read. Their speech became crude.
Their manners sometimes offensive. It was the penalty they had to pay" [*SE*]. In
Paterson Williams remembers Pound's taunt: "Your interest is in the bloody loam
but what / I'm after is the finished product." The finished product, he would
answer, can only come from the bloody loam, but, like the hunters who pushed
beyond the settlers and were lost in the wilderness, the new American poet may
become so imbedded in the earth that he is speechless or speaks indistinctly and
so ineffectively: "It is imperative that we *sink*. But from a low position it is impossible to answer those who know all the Latin and some of the Sanskrit names,
much French and perhaps one or two other literatures. . . . [W]here foreign values
are held to be a desideratum, he who is buried and speaks thickly—is lost. . . .
Those who come up from under will have a mark on them that invites scorn, like
a farmer's filthy clodhoppers" [*IAG*]. "I am far under them," he says in *The
Great American Novel*. "I am less, far less if you will. I am a beginner." The
achievement of form of whatever sort is subject to a double jeopardy. If the
generative urge remains buried in the earth it is not form at all, "no syllable in
the confused / uproar" [*P*], no flower in the shapeless mud, but as soon as it rises
altogether free of the ground it becomes a hollow shell.

What vitality disappears? If the earth is just earth, it ought to be possible to give it a permanent form, create a fixed culture which would be valid forever. Why is it that, "unless there is / a new mind there cannot be a new / line, the old will go on / repeating itself with recurring / deadliness" [P]? Why is form false unless, like Antaeus, it keeps touch with the earth?

The answer is that third element, the "hidden flame" [IAG] present in the ground but invisible, and present too in every form but covered up as soon as the form gets fixed in a shape. Only in the moment when the flower rises from the ground is a brief glimpse of the presence released. For this reason validity lies in the process of flowering and not in the flower full blown. Every birth is an uncovering of the secret, but as soon as the child is assimilated into the already existing human community, the flame is shaded, the unique is reduced to common measure: "Thus the birth of every baby, whatever its quality, is a revelation. But the moment it is christened, circumcised or indoctrinated by other means into whatever sect or clan will delimit it from others of its generation, revelation is at an end" [SE]. Only when the child and its source are still in living relation is the presence manifest. Authenticity lies in a present moment which moves and changes as form emerges from the shapeless origin. The image of flowering, constantly appearing in Williams's work, is the opening out of the real in the fleeting moment of uncovering before things are dead and fixed. As objects rise from the ground and blossom, the delicate perfume of beauty is released. So, in a good poem "the sentence lives, the movement lives, the object flares up (out of the dark). That is what I mean by reality, it lives again (as always) in our day." In the same way, "each serious American writer in turn," like an object in a poem, "flares up for a moment and fizzles out, burnt out by the air" [GAN].

THOMAS R. WHITAKER

New Worlds

The New World presses on us all; there seems no end to it—and no beginning.

During the 1920s Williams explored new worlds in four prose works: *The Great American Novel* (1923), *In the American Grain* (1925), *A Voyage to Pagany* (1928), and *January: A Novelette* (1929; published 1932). Though all except *A Voyage to Pagany* have usually been called "impressionistic essays," their central meanings appear most clearly if we attend to their structures as prose fictions. One of them, *In the American Grain*, ranks with *Paterson* as a major achievement. The others, though less firmly realized, are valuable renderings of an alert mind's continual renewal of contact—with itself, its changing environment, and its historical ground.

I. THE GREAT AMERICAN NOVEL

The Great American Novel is a seventy-page, ironic fulfillment of a common literary ambition during the first part of this century. Its first chapter, "The Fog," opens with distinctively American buoyance: "If there is progress then there is a novel." But the writer immediately encounters difficulties. Progress implies a beginning, and how does one begin a work that presumes to confront the new? At what point in time? And by constructing with words—as Mallarmé had advised Degas—or with immediate sensations? By forging a radically new style or by rendering the present through a workmanlike realism? The content, of course, must be new—but a new baby, a dynamo, an obscene word, a grotesque cripple? Such problems are serious enough, but the voice that poses them (heard through

From *William Carlos Williams.* © 1968 by Twayne Publishers, Inc., a division of G. K. Hall & Co., Boston.

the pervasive fog) is now elated, now confused, now slipping into fatuousness, and now parodying itself:

> That which had been impossible for him at first had become possible. Everything had been removed that other men had tied to the words to secure them to themselves. Clean, clean he had taken each word and made it new for himself so that at last it was new, free from the world for himself—never to touch it—dreams of his babyhood —poetic sweetheart. No. He went in to his wife with exalted mind, his breath coming in pleasant surges. I come to tell you that the book is finished.
>
> I have added a new chapter to the art of writing. I feel sincerely that all they say of me is true, that I am truly a great man and a great poet.
>
> What did you say, dear, I have been asleep?

So ends Chapter 2, climaxing a sequence that has slyly subverted item after item in Williams's own literary program. That sequence is not (as it may at points have seemed) a writer's diary or a ground-clearing operation preliminary to the novel itself; it is the first section of a fiction that will dramatize how contact becomes plunder, the clean becomes the null, and the new becomes the sham. *The Great American Novel* paints that web of dreams, pretensions, discoveries, and betrayals which constitutes the New World. It must therefore begin by dramatizing the comparable web in the mind of any writer who would render his New World.

Of course, the "beginning" sought by this first Williams *persona* is never found. *His* novel is never written: there is no plot, and there are no characters. What does emerge is perhaps not *a* novel ("a thing of fixed form") but something that is continually novel—not a "progress" but what Williams would later call "a progression" [*Selected Essays* (New York: Random House, 1954)]. Its own "new world"—composed by sympathetically and sardonically examining many other "new worlds"—is a moment-by-moment alertness to the possibilities of discovery and stultification. To see this work as "a confession of inadequacy" is to miss its main thrust. Its real subject is immediacy of contact; and— like the later works of this decade—it is a fiction of many voices.

After working through the more obvious vacuities that trap a writer who seeks to confront the New World, the fiction moves closer (in Chapter 3) to the actual voice of Williams: "It is Joyce with a difference. The difference being greater opacity, less erudition, reduced power of perception." The self-parody now becomes subtler; the dialogues with alter-egos become more pointed. "Take the improvisations: What the French reader would say is *Oui, ça; j'ai déjà vu ça; ça c'est de Rimbaud"* —exactly what Pound had told Williams. And this chapter can close with a dialogue that renders no dream of lofty accomplishment but a readiness to descend and inquire:

> —To me beauty is purity. To me it is discovery, a race on the ground.
> And for this you are willing to smash—
> Yes, everything. —To go down into hell. —Well let's look.

The following chapters continue such dialogue, interspersed with broader parody. As the Williams *persona* insists that everything "must be re-valued" and rejects any mere complication of consciousness, his antagonist becomes a definitely European voice—and the fog becomes a drenching rain. Williams has emerged into some clarity of intent, a passion for accuracy and articulation that is rendered in the contrasting rhythms and intonations of the two voices:

> But you poor fellow, you use such inept figures. Aida has been dead artistically in Munich for fifty years.
> Wagner then—Strauss. It is no difference to me. Tear it all apart. Start with one note. One word. Chant it over and over forty different ways.
> But it would be stupid—
> It would, if it were what I mean—it would be accurate.

Chapter 6 modulates into a lightly ironic portrait of America and the American writer. The sun returns, and the fecundating and destroying wind (emblem of change, of the writer and the betrayer) begins to frolic. The chapter's conclusion echoes that of Chapter 2, but with a light detachment: "Quietly he goes home to his wife and taking her by the shoulder wakes her: Here I am." And with that simple announcement, the mode of discovery ("let's look") has been reached.

Now the dreams, pretensions, and betrayals of the writer recede; those of his New World become the main theme. Chapters 7 through 10 present a series of ironically juxtaposed images: Columbus's discovery (in ignorance of Eric the Discoverer); children playing amid newly fallen leaves; the writer wondering if it is too late to be Eric; Indians and Villistas rebelling against their new-world masters; Mormon pioneers insisting on a fixed truth, dominating, betraying, and prospering; Aaron Burr on his wedding day; De Soto contemplating the Mississippi—and many more. Occasional summaries may use explicit statement —"*Nuevo Mundo*, shouted the sailors. But their cry was by now almost extinct" —or more densely symbolic montage: "Oh my country. Shall it be a hysterectomy? Arnold there is a wind with a knife's edge." In context, this focuses a complex wind of change—ambition, corruption, loss of fertility—from Revolutionary to modern times. To paint the background of American life is, in several senses, "painting the wind."

As the panorama widens, we see flamboyance and art denied, leading to deformity and crime. The New World becomes De Soto's river of dissolution, inhabited by scavenging fish. We also learn another reason why *The Great American Novel* can have no "beginning" and no "progress." Time is mere "superstition": the "eternal moment" remains "twining in its hair the flowers of yesterday and tomorrow." Though history is process, it repeats in new forms a universal condition, balancing evolution and involution. How can a style render such paradoxes? "Davy Crockett had a literary style. Rather than blow his squirrel to bits he'd strike the tree just under its belly so that the concussion would stun it. Such was the country with the element of time subtracted." This is the rationale for Williams's own non-temporal inventories or montages.

By Chapter 17 Williams can include more sustained documentary passages, for we now can place their qualities with reference to the alertness enacted by the book's total structure. In an account of Cumberland Mountain women, filtered through a style that ranges from ingratiating clichés to precise observations, we glimpse a love of beauty and a natural sanity—but also hardship, defeat, and inertia. Ma Duncan's sad comment (like the Evangelist's sermon in *Paterson*) is an ironically naïve version of what needs to be said: "I wish you could have seen the great old trees that used to be here. If folks wasn't so mad for money they might be here and a preachin' the gospel of beauty. But folks is all for money and all for self."

A coda to the chapter, pointing up the idealizing haze of the foregoing travelogue, dryly summarizes a news report of a pastor who has just returned from Buffalo, dramatically repentant for having strayed there with a member of his flock. That bit of Americana serves as transition to the success stories of Chapter 18, which lead on toward the rain of the final chapter and its last two voices—those of the bland organization man, maker of syringes and thermometers, and the efficient maker of shoddy, envious of someone else who can clear a million on cheap quilts or invent a fake oilcloth: "Nothing but building paper with a coating of enamel."

From fog to shoddy, from slick words to slick enamel—it is indeed a New World. The "progression" of *The Great American Novel* exhibits the meaning of those ambitions, those self-expansive and possessive movements, that are implicit in its title. Such qualities are part of what it is to be an American, maker and discoverer of the "new." As Williams later commented, "I do want to *say* what there is. It is not for me merely to arrange things prettily" [*Selected Letters*, ed. Thirlwall (New York: McDowell, Obolensky, 1957)]. And in saying what there is, *The Great American Novel* enacts another kind of "new world": a genuine making and discovering, a verbal dance of self-measurement over the body of the American's ironic condition.

II. IN THE AMERICAN GRAIN

In 1920 D. H. Lawrence had addressed the readers of the *New Republic* with the words: "America, Listen to Your Own." As Americans move toward fulfillment of their unrevealed destiny, he said, they must turn for support not to the perfected monuments of the European past—which have an "almost fatal narcotic, dream-luxurious effect upon the soul"—but to whatever in their own dark continent is "unresolved" and "rejected." "That which was abhorrent to the Pilgrim Fathers and to the Spaniards, that which was called the Devil, the black Demon of savage America, this great aboriginal spirit the Americans must recognize again, recognize and embrace." Lawrence was asking for no facile romanticism but a "mysterious, delicate process" of establishing contact with all in oneself that is unresolved and rejected, and, in so doing, stepping beyond fixation upon a dead past and a defensive partiality. This understanding of psychic integration—very close to Williams's own understanding of "descent"—lies behind what otherwise might be mere admiration of the noble savage: "Americans must take up life where the Red Indian, the Aztec, the Maya, the Incas left it off. . . . They must catch the pulse of the life which Cortés and Columbus murdered. There lies the real continuity: not between Europe and the new States, but between the murdered Red America and the seething white America." Lawrence urged that this theme—touched upon "uncannily, unconsciously," in the past—now become fully conscious: Americans "must be ready for a new act, a new extension of life."

Lawrence's own detailed support for this exhortation, already partly set forth in the *English Review* during 1918-19, appeared in 1923 as *Studies in Classic American Literature*. And in the same year came the first major American response—Williams's series of pieces in *Broom* which, two years later, were collected as part of *In the American Grain*. The rapidity of Williams's response (as well as a good deal of internal evidence) suggests his acquaintance with Lawrence's essays in the *English Review*. In 1918 Williams had also written, "The New World is Montezuma," and he had imagined a descent to Tenochtitlán [*Kora in Hell: Improvisations* (San Francisco: City Lights, 1957)]. In any case, *In the American Grain* subtly enacts the movement toward which Lawrence pointed: it renders in its structure one version of that "mysterious, delicate process" of embrace and integration.

Williams later gave [in his *Autobiography*] three partial definitions of his intent: to "try to get inside the heads of some of the American founders . . . by examining their original records"; to "make each chapter not only in content but in the style itself a close study of the theme"; and to "draw from every source one thing, the strange phosphorus of the life, nameless under an old misappellation." But the work's more inclusive meaning appears only if we add to such definitions the principle of dialogue or conversation. In theme and in style, *In the American Grain* is a dialogical encounter with the New World.

Unlike an "objective" historian, Williams does not try to eliminate himself from his study; but neither does he merely reduce whatever he finds to an illustration of some present thesis or feeling. He sometimes listens very closely, reproducing long documents verbatim or allowing his own style to become a delicate pastiche. In so doing, he may discover certain configurations of the past and also clues to his own hidden nature; and he may thus create a "historical" character who can speak with a double life. Or again, he may step back to contemplate a wider historical pattern—and may then debate with himself and with others, move from one position to another, and examine his own impulses toward historical encounter.

Such a process—the continuing "impact of the bare soul upon the very twist of the fact," self-revising and self-elucidating—leads, of course, to no neat pattern of objective details. Williams had already rejected that kind of self-deceptive history in 1918: "Of course history is an attempt to make the past seem stable and of course it's all a lie. Nero must mean Nero or the game's up." And he had hinted there ("Confute the sages") at his own very different project [*Kora*]. *In the American Grain* presents history not as result but as process. Because history is *now*—alive or dead in a present mind—any fixed idea of the past is a fixation in oneself. That is why Williams urges: "History must stay open, it is all humanity." In accord with that view, *In the American Grain* is a conversation of many voices, dramatizing the continuing discovery (of the past and of oneself) that may occur as a man pays attention to his historical ground.

The first voice, that of Williams as Red Eric, is clearly fictional. It is as though the alienated and self-alienated speakers of "Portrait of a Woman in Bed" and "Dedication for a Plot of Ground" had discovered in the style and content of Norse saga an ancestral tongue. And Eric's self-portrait can therefore sum up many facets of the ironic American predicament to be developed in this book. Eric is exile and discoverer, victim and murderer, possessor of clean strength and ruthless simplifier, relisher of the new and perpetuator of his own curse. In his own laconic mode, he points toward Columbus, Montezuma, Washington, Burr, Poe, and others. But before this first study is complete, there enters a second voice—a terse saga voice describing a fateful historical continuity. "So, thinning out, more and more dark, it ran: Eric in Freydis's bones." From sympathetic and ironic identification with Eric we have stepped back to a contemplative vantage-point within his own time.

It is but one more step to the third voice, that of Williams as historian, which opens "The Discovery of the Indies" with another modulation of the theme:

> The New World, existing in those times beyond the sphere of all things known to history, lay in the fifteenth century as the middle of the desert or the sea lies now and must lie forever, marked with its own dark life which goes on to an immaculate fulfillment in which we have no part. But now, with the maritime successes of that period, the western land could not guard its seclusion longer; a predestined and bitter fruit existing, perversely, before the white flower of its birth, it was laid bare by the miraculous first voyage. For it is as the achievement of a flower, pure, white, waxlike and fragrant, that Columbus's infatuated course must be depicted, especially when compared with the acrid and poisonous apple which was later by him to be proved.

Now the counterpoint of voices becomes more rapid and ironic. Columbus speaks in his own person, the voice of obsessive and doomed action; Williams, as historian, comments from a contemplative distance upon the pattern of the discoverer's heroic course. And this counterpoint prepares for the chapter's remarkable conclusion. Columbus's statements are arranged so as to dramatize the perverse teleology hinted in the opening paragraph: Williams follows the first voyage, leaps over the moment of initial discovery, and then gives the "predestined and bitter fruit"; only then does he lead back toward the "white flower of its birth": "But if, as he instinctively, but for his insane doggedness, would have done, he had undertaken that holy pilgrimage of which he had spoken, the flower might again, in that seclusion, often have appeared to him in all its old-time loveliness, as when he himself floated with luck and in sunshine on that tropic sea toward adventure and discovery.

Then follows Columbus's account of the moment of initial discovery. But this "white flower" is presented by a strangely double voice. It is, of course, the literal voice of first discovery; but, because of its placement in the contrapuntal pattern, it is also the voice of a retrospective contemplation that Columbus did not allow himself to know. The voices merge: that of Columbus, as agent and potential contemplator, joins that of Williams, as contemplator and imaginative agent.

In "The Destruction of Tenochtitlan" the historian's voice comes into its own. Yvor Winters has said that Williams merely "*happened* to write a twelve-page masterpiece" in the traditional heroic prose that Macaulay "*chose*" for his five-volume *History*. On the contrary, this is the one piece which, because of its content and its position in the dialectical sequence of voices, demands heroic treatment. It focuses the full destructive engagement of our double inheritance. Our qualified sympathy with the explorers—Eric and Columbus—must now be more fully called into question as Cortéz meets Montezuma. And the dark "fate" hinted earlier must now be probed more deeply: "Upon the orchidean beauty of the new world the old rushed inevitably to revenge itself after the Italian's return. Such things occur in secret. Though men may be possessed by beauty while they work that is all they know of its or their own terrible hands; they do not fathom the forces which carry them."

No political, economic, or religious explanation of the ravaging of the new world will suffice: "It was the spirit of malice which underlies men's lives and against which nothing offers resistance. And bitter as the thought may be that Tenochtitlán, the barbaric city, its people, its genius wherever found should have been crushed out because of the awkward names men give their emptiness, yet it was no man's fault. It was the force of the pack whom the dead drive."

Ignorant of that force, the Spanish are driven on from discovery to plunder in a feverish desire to fill their emptiness. More aware of that force, the Aztecs make "a ceremonial acknowledgment of the deep sexless urge of life itself, the hungry animal, underlying all other power; the mysterious secret of existence whose cruel beauty they, the living, inherited from the dead." They recognize in their sculpture that the "earth is black and it is there: only art advances." Here, as in "Red Eric," historical accuracy is a secondary matter; we need not debate the nature of the Aztec flowering from its basis in an "earthward thrust" or the reasons for Montezuma's vacillating response to Cortéz. Williams richly presents, through the forms of the past, a perennially possible human conflict. The delicate surface of a culture that has lifted itself above the "isolate blackness" of savagery is crushed by another manifestation of that savagery—one which, considering itself more civilized, is ignorant of its own meanings.

The voice which presents this conflict with such balance and sweep—a voice not of blame but of impartial and ironic recognition, with an undercurrent of pathos—comes to us as itself a dialectical synthesis of the opposing forces. Through that voice Williams acknowledges his own inheritance of violent hunger in its European forms. And the writing is therefore at one with the Aztec achievement whose downfall it describes. The dark earthward thrust has been recognized, and art flowers—even as, stylistically, these sombre recognitions shape a delicate texture within the Aztec cut-block paragraphs.

However, even that heroic style imposes a distorting form upon our human response to the conflict. That is why the next piece, "The Fountain of Eternal Youth," must enact a balancing movement:

History, history! We fools, what do we know or care? History begins
for us with murder and enslavement, not with discovery. No, we
are not Indians but we are men of their world. . . . These are the
inhabitants of our souls, our murdered souls that lie . . . agh. Listen! I
tell you it was lucky for Spain the first ship put its men ashore where
it did. If the Italian had landed in Florida, one twist of the helm
north, or among the islands a hair more to the south; among the
Yemasses with their sharpened bones and fishspines, or among the
Caribs with their poisoned darts—it might have begun differently.

This informal voice, closer to the spontaneous voice of the actual writer, can
more fully express sympathies that have earlier been held in partial abeyance.
Williams moves yet further toward that "embrace" of which Lawrence had
written—but without denying his European identity: "We are, too, the others.
. . . We are the slaughterers." Style and content descend from the heroic to the
folk: snatches of proverb and song weave in and out of the prose as the *fata
morgana* of the New World, now incarnate in an old slave-woman, tempts the
all-too-human Ponce to his death. The ironic conclusion of "The Destruction of
Tenochtitlan"—"*Viva quien vence!*"—is answered by the exultantly laconic full
stop of this more personal account: "Dead."

After exploring the self as implicit in both terms of the historical conflict,
the style of *In the American Grain* now explicitly enacts the thrust and oblique
counterthrust—the sexual jiu-jitsu—whereby the feminine New World helps its
masculine vanquishers toward their own destruction. In the counterpoint of "De
Soto and the New World" the voice of that New World ("She") replaces the
historian's commentary on Columbus; and a pastiche of contemporary narrative
replaces the first-person voice of the explorer. This method of narration means a
somewhat greater distance from both author and explorer, but also a clearer
dramatic conflict and historical perspective as De Soto moves to his final descent
into the body of the Mississippi River, his appetite translated by the sardonic
logic of history into the gross symbols of fish and hogs.

As "Sir Walter Raleigh" develops that sexual encounter on a fuller historical and geographical scale, the insane doggedness of action now merges stylistically with the contemplative release in a single voice—that of Williams as
quasi-Elizabethan poet: "Of the pursuit of beauty and the husk that remains,
perversions and mistakes, while the true form escapes in the wind, sing O Muse;
of Raleigh, beloved by majesty, plunging his lust into the body of a new world—
and the deaths, misfortunes, counter coups which swelled back to certify that
ardor with defeat."

This mode catches Raleigh in "the mesh of his own period's forms" [*Selected Letters*]—doing ironic justice to his wide-ranging intellect and appetite,

his lyricism and common sense, his infatuation and emptiness—"his England become a mouthful of smoke sucked from the embers of a burnt weed." As celebration, it can include Raleigh's own unexperienced "white flower"—the discovery of an idyllic Virginia; and, as dialogue with the Muse, it can move finally to those bitter doubts that a modern inquirer must entertain: "Question him in hell, O Muse, where he has gone, and when there is an answer, sing and make clear the reasons that he gave for that last blow. Why did he send his son into that tropic jungle and not go himself, upon so dangerous an errand? And when the boy had died why not die too? Why England again and force the new King to keep his promise and behead him?" The last meaning of the conventionally heroic mode—here as everywhere—is its ironic lack of heroism.

In "Voyage of the Mayflower" Williams once more returns from heroic flight to a contemporary voice which may vent a more immediate sadness and animus, as he considers the "seed of lusty Tudor England's blossoming." Exiled and lost, fearful of individuality, the Puritans perpetuate as a curse that hardness and littleness which enabled them to survive: "it is still to-day the Puritan who keeps his frightened grip on the throat of the world lest it should prove him—empty." For Williams in the 1920s, as for Lawrence, Puritanism is the most alarmingly murderous contemporary force—an "atavism" that causes souls to perish miserably or bends them into "grotesque designs of violence and despair." But the rhetorical violence, into which this theme betrays Williams, clearly testifies to an intensity of feeling not yet understood. As Williams later recognizes, the discussion of Puritanism is the least alert portion of *In The American Grain*.

As these three pieces have modulated from De Soto to Raleigh and then to the Puritans, the next three modulate from Champlain to Thomas Morton and then to Cotton Mather. "The Founding of Quebec" recognizes yet more fully the inadequacy of any single form or voice as a means of rendering a full human response to history. Here the dialogue, seemingly between two friends, is really between projected facets of Williams himself. The first speaker loses himself in admiration for Champlain, "the perfection of what we lack, here." He sees not Parkman's "man all for the theme and purpose, nothing for himself," but a man who is "all for himself—but gently, with love, with patience." He stresses his "tenderness," and his "love of the exact detail," but also his "tremendous energy" and adventurousness.

The first speaker's insistence upon Champlain's living presence might almost render the position of *In the American Grain* as a whole: "Here was a man. Here *is* a man after my own heart. Is it merely in a book? So am I then, merely in a book." But a wry truth in this last sentence gradually becomes apparent: if Champlain is all for himself, this speaker is all for an imagined Champlain. No wonder this speaker so readily understands Machiavelli's practice of

dressing himself for a new part as he enters his study! At some point the historical imagination has become, for him, an escape. And there is a disturbing affinity
between the Old World delicacy which he admires and his own merely literary
mode of admiration. This temptation, of course, inheres in Williams's entire
mode of procedure; but, dramatizing the temptation, this conversation can move
beyond it.

The friend's reply—in a brusque Williams voice of another order—may
seem rudely unwarranted by the historical details offered earlier. But it is the
necessary counterpoint to the first speaker's actual position: "To hell with all
that: collecting pictures for France—or science—or art! What for the New
World? No. I know what you mean. A spirit of resignation. Literature. Books—
a library. Good night, then. That's not you." And he tersely develops his own
thesis, the failure of France against the New World's savagery: "a force to leap
up and wrench you from your hold and force you to be part of it; the place,
the absolute new without a law but the basic blood where the savage becomes
brother. That is generous. Open. A break through. Champlain couldn't." If the
friend's final plea is desperately romantic—"The land! don't you feel it? Doesn't
it make you want to go out and lift dead Indians tenderly from their graves, to
steal from them—as if it must be clinging even to their corpses—some authenticity, that which—" —he nonetheless breaks off and concludes with a phrase
that does accurately sum up his meaning: "Here not there."

The structure of *In the American Grain* recognizes and moves beyond both
the subtle and the crude error, both the literary admiration and the violent and
equally sentimental counter-assertion of "land" and "savagery." The volume's
own "position"—a living process—emerges from such dialogue. Its direction is
already apparent in the fact that both debaters about Champlain would move
toward the attentive, the constructive, the generous, the strong. Though grounds
for historical pessimism remain, *In the American Grain* now searches for a mode
of action adequate to a full humanity: one consistent with (and, indeed, stem-
ming from) that state of contemplation which, in the opening pieces, transcended
the infatuated careers of the first explorers. The historian of "The Destruction of
Tenochtitlan" could say, "The earth is black and it is there: only art advances."
But the question now is: May not a life that is in touch with the imagination also
advance, somehow, into the open?

More directly engaging the dialogue of historians among themselves, "The
May-Pole at Merry Mount" views from another angle the open and the closed
as contemporary states of mind. Williams protests the "nearly universal lack of
scale" in writings on American history, shows how a modern scholar's paro-
chialism and complacent humor may be like Puritan narrowness, and concludes
with a pointed contrast in modes of touch:

As Morton laid his hands, roughly perhaps but lovingly, upon the
flesh of his Indian consorts, so the Puritans laid theirs with malice,
with envy, insanely, not only upon him, but also—one thing leading
to another—upon the unoffending Quakers.

Trustless of humane experience, not knowing what to think, they
went mad, lost all direction. Mather defends the witchcraft perse-
cutions.

And then Williams prudently lapses into silence, for the next piece, "Cotton
Mather's Wonders of the Invisible World," quite simply allows Mather to con-
vict himself out of his own mouth.

"Père Sebastian Rasles," the central piece of the book, dramatically places
Williams's own endeavor as historian, with reference to both American and
European contexts. The dialogue, probing and testing Williams's response to history more fully than has hitherto been possible, now involves no fictional projection but another live person—the sensitive and scholarly Valéry Larbaud. Williams must wryly admit that, compared with Larbaud, he has not really read
Mather ("I had *seen* the book and brushed through its pages hunting for something I wished to verify"), and that his anti-Puritanism has something of the
Puritanical ("Fiery particles, the Puritans, I said, acquainting him with my rigid
tenet"). And he presents Larbaud's intelligent awareness of the remoteness of
those Catholic and Protestant influences and the obsessive quality of Williams's
own struggle: "Very well, he assented, you are from that place. You are caught
by a smell. It is good that you struggle to appreciate it. . . . Mather. *What* a
force, still to interest you; it is admirable. But I find your interest 'très théorique.' "
But Williams has two answers to that last judgment: first, the portrayal of Rasles,
the Jesuit priest, who is no theory but a man, "a moral source not reckoned
with, peculiarly sensitive and daring in its close embrace of native things"; the
second, this dialogue itself, which is no theoretical presentation but a dramatic
working-through of an existential situation.

More fully than any character thus far, Rasles embodies what is necessary
for growth in the New World; a mode of action springing from attentive contact.
Living with the Indians, accepting their hardships, admiring their qualities (even
their warfare, though he has no need to fight himself), touching them daily—he
seems that Lawrentian "embrace": "It is *this* to be *moral*: to be positive, to be
peculiar, to be sure, generous, brave—TO MARRY, to *touch*,—to *give* because
one HAS, not because one has nothing." In contrast to the Puritanical blocking
of all approach to the "tenderer humanities," Williams postulates a Catholicism
that (after a "blow on the head") "comes at least with gentleness to aid."

The removal of intellectual difficulty by authority "leaves hands freed for
embraces, a field where tenderness may move, love may awaken and (save by the

one blocked door) a way is offered." But the immediate context of this celebration —a talk between Williams and a French intellectual—stresses the ironic importance of that one blocked door. Nevertheless, the positive relevance of all that Rasles embodies is also stressed by the Parisian context of self-encysted exiles. "I felt myself with ardors not released but beaten back," Williams had said, "in this center of old-world culture where everyone was tearing his own meat, *warily* conscious of a new-comer, but wholly without inquisitiveness— No wish to know; they were served."

That metaphor of food, in fact, runs through the chapter; and it helps to define the various modes of contact and assimilation, from English plunder (the New World "a carcass from which to tear pieces for their belly's sake") through Larbaud's more refined intellectual appetite and Williams's search for sustenance ("Have you not yourself proven that there is meat—Yes . . . the early records— to try to find—something, a freshness"), and on to Rasles's mode of being, as a spirit "able to give and to receive, full of taste, a nose, a tongue," whose acts were therefore "luscious fruit" and whose letters are even now "a river that brings sweet water to us."

It is clearly a "source" in the fullest sense that this dialogical movement now seeks; and a native source is found in "The Discovery of Kentucky." Debating with the writer of Daniel Boone's so-called autobiography (and with the anonymous authors of the Boone legend generally), Williams sets up his own image of a "great voluptuary" and solitary who descended "to the ground of his desire." "Passionate and thoroughly given he avoided the half logic of stealing from the immense profusion." Boone saw that the difficulty in the New World was "purely moral and aesthetic," that there "must be a new wedding," and that the necessary prototype was the "native savage": "Not for himself surely to be an Indian, though they eagerly sought to adopt him into their tribes, but the reverse: to be himself in a new world, Indian-like."

As complementary figures, Rasles and Boone focus those qualities which *In the American Grain* has thus far discovered as most consonant with its own humane contact with sources: a passionate self-giving and concomitant receiving through touch. Against the background of that discovery, the book can now explore—in Washington, Franklin, John Paul Jones, modern women (as contrasted with Jacataqua), Burr, the Negroes, Houston, Poe, and Lincoln—various blockages and perversions, pathetically limited openings and escapes, desperate descents beneath the crust of a culture gone wrong, and attempts to sustain or focus its fragmentary pattern. Of these explorations, I select three for some comment.

The piece on Aaron Burr, "The Virtue of History," is one of the most illuminatingly paradoxical dialogues in the book. And, aside from the total pattern of *In the American Grain*, it is the best refutation of the charge that "it seems never to occur to Williams that some secrets must always be kept from the historian." As one of two speakers, Williams discards all received interpretations of history as mere ways of imprisoning the dead "within some narrow definition." "No opinion can be trusted; . . . but if a verdict be unanimous, it is sure to be a wrong one, a crude rush of the herd which has carried its object before it like a helpless condoning image."

However, if we must discard the fixed, we need not remain barrenly contemplating the unknowable; we must consider the possibility that the as-yet-unknown may correspond to something in our own sense of hidden potential life. Only in this way may an open history sustain an open life in the present. "That of the dead which exists in our imaginations has as much fact as have we ourselves. The premise that serves to fix us fixes also that part of them which we remember." When such intellectual freezing occurs, history tyrannizes over the "imaginations of the living—where lies our greatest well of inspiration, our greatest hope of freedom." For "men, never content in the malice with which they surround each living moment, must extend their illwill backward, jealous even of a freedom in the past, to maim and to destroy there too."

In accord with that necessary openness, Williams sets forth his own view of Burr. His friend, the other speaker in the dialogue, presses for factual substantiation, which Williams is hard put to provide. But his difficulty does not finally matter: he at least has fended off the usual view of Burr as vain, treacherous, profligate, selfish. And his own view, unproved but suggestive, symbolizes exactly what he finds in an open history: he sees in Burr a "humanity, his own, free and independent, unyielding to the herd, practical, direct," and an awareness that (against all leveling by the mass mind with its fixed systems) democracy must liberate men "intact—with all their senses waking." It is this vitality that lives in the man's "style."

The friend, appropriately enough, remains unconvinced. He finally comments: "But passion will obscure our sense so that we eat sad stuff and call it nectar." And perhaps he is right: Williams may have been so deceived. But Williams's own oblique response is also appropriate: an anecdote that proves nothing but stresses Burr's own awareness of the tyranny of mob opinion. The dialogue thus recognizes the possibility of self-deception (and thereby prevents such self-deception from being disabling) even while it allows Williams to discern in these historical forms a "hidden flame" that "cannot be packed into three common words." Against all that is closed or whittled down he urges the *possibility* of this life: "He's in myself and so I dig through lies to resurrect him."

In the context of this dialogical recognition of the need for openness and the possibility of self-deception, that statement is ample justification for the historical fictions of *In the American Grain*. History must be "a living thing, something moving, undecided, swaying . . . something on the brink of the Unknown." In it, the alert mind may discover its own new movements of growth. Rendered in art, these movements may be liberating for others. That is why Williams can say that only in "the hands of the stylist, literature," is humanity "protected against tyrannous designs."

Thus forewarned, we may read "Edgar Allan Poe," a sustained answer to the conventional view of that poet, as a comparable resurrection of something in Williams. Here he finds what it is to be a poet in the New World. Delving beneath the surface phenomenon—the macabre genius, "lost upon the grotesque and the arabesque"—he finds "a necessity for a fresh beginning" and a deep torment caused by the immediate effect of America's overwhelming profusion of the makeshift and the colossal. Poe was a new De Soto and a new Eric: "Rather the ice than their way." His gesture was "to BE CLEAN." And the detailed account of his attack upon the language—a labor to detach something clear from the "inchoate mass"—is often an apt description of Williams's own endeavor.

The very strains involved in readjusting our view of Poe in this manner are salutary: a study of Whitman at this point would have merely reinforced our view of a conventional and dead past. Through Poe's distinctive kind of "localism," his awareness of "the possibility, the sullen, volcanic inevitability of the *place*," Williams prevents our misunderstanding of what it means to marry the New World. The feeling in Poe's tales is "a local one, surely, but not of sentiment or mood, as not of trees and Indians, but of original fibre, the normal toughness which fragility of mood presupposes, if it will be expressive of anything." In such sentences, *In the American Grain* reveals the inner meaning of its earlier images.

Williams had spoken of his own "brutalizing battle" to hear himself "above the boilermakers in and about New York"; now he finds the "wraithlike quality" of Poe's lyrics to result from the same predicament: "Poe stayed against the thin edge, driven to be heard by the battering racket about him to a distant screaming —the pure essence of his locality." But Williams's own quite different fate we may read more clearly in three other prophetic comments. There is, first, the saving gesture which will become the climax of *Paterson* 4: "His greatness is in that he turned his back and faced inland, to originality, with the identical gesture of a Boone." Second, there is a clue to the structure of that later poem: the "secret" of Poe's method in the tales, we are told, is "authentic particles, a thousand of which spring to the mind for quotation, taken apart and reknit with a view to emphasize, enforce and make evident, the *method*. . . . The whole period, America 1840, could be rebuilt, psychologically (phrenologically) from Poe's 'method.' " And, third, there is a comment on the poetry which points to a transformation implicit in much of Williams's work but especially evident in his own last poems: "It is not by a change in character but by its quickened motion that it has turned from mere heat into light—by its power of penetration that it has been brought to dwell upon love. By its acid power to break down truth that it has been *forced* upon love."

Indeed, those sentences also suggest the concluding direction of Williams's dialogue with American history in this volume. The coda, "Abraham Lincoln," is a startling but poignant prose poem which fixes in a series of images the "brutalizing desolation of life in America" and its perverse "flowering." Under the maternally presiding Lincoln, the dialogical process within the country became a strange orchestration of isolate voices: "The violins, surrounded, yet feel that they have come alone, in silence and in secret, singly to be heard." The "age-old torture" had reached a "disastrous climax." And, in describing that climax, the last two sentences of *In the American Grain* succeed in pointing obliquely to its own orchestration and its own understanding of a historical process that must continue into an open future: "Failing of relief or expression, the place tormented itself into a convulsion of bewilderment and pain—with a woman, born somehow, aching over it, holding all fearfully together. It was the end of THAT period."

III. A VOYAGE TO PAGANY

Because the New World exists in no single time or place, Williams's next fiction can discover it through a descent into the Old World. In fact, *A Voyage to Pagany* is the necessary counterpoint to *The Great American Novel* and *In the American Grain*; it enacts for Williams another loosening, descent, and reintegration, re-establishing contact with what has been unresolved and rejected during several years of frequently insistent Americanism. Biographically, of course, the phases of this process cannot be so neatly distinguished: *A Voyage to Pagany* closely follows the itinerary of Williams's European trip of 1924; and parts of *In the American Grain*—most notably the conversation with Valéry Larbaud—had already benefited from that balancing movement. Williams had said of the man who has understood what it is to "descend": "If he goes to France, it is not to learn a *do re mi fa sol*. He goes to see a strange New World." But now Williams explores the meaning of that fact. His Dr. Evans of New Jersey, as he enters Europe and the European past, is nonetheless making a live step forward: "He felt the old clarity overlaid, he felt that he wanted to go on—to that. . . . Greece is ahead of us, not back."

In detail, his voyage of discovery is a very uneven work: it includes much imperfectly assimilated material; the minor characters are not fully realized; and the story line is often abrupt and arbitrary. However, its symbolic progression is generally convincing, and it contains many forceful sequences. Although the theme of the American discovering himself in Europe may seem rather Jamesian, the prose is frequently in a modified Joycean telegraphic style, and the psychological pattern most significantly recalls D. H. Lawrence. Like the protagonists of *Kangaroo*, *St. Mawr*, or *The Plumed Serpent*, Evans descends from the rigidities of an established life and a home culture to traverse a shadowily populated and historically potent landscape that constellates in projected form all in himself with which he needs renewed acquaintance. Indeed, *A Voyage to Pagany* is yet closer to Lawrence's own travel books—especially *Twilight in Italy* and *Mornings in Mexico*—which dramatize similar psychological descents.

At life's midpoint, Evans leaves that America which has shaped itself about him as an island of the known and (in a fashion that recalls the Heinesque motifs of *Kora in Hell*) encounters a sea and a continent which are now for him "home of the wild gods in exile." As he travels to Paris, the Riviera, Italy, and Austria, the shifting scenes vividly register his continuing abandonment of the known and his discovery of the age-old new. And a series of encounters with other Americans, each of whom seems in some way a "curious variant of himself," expands the meaning of his journey. Each has made a partial and limiting adjustment to Europe and to his own deeper being—fixing upon some portion of what has been revealed or released, or yet more pathetically settling for some flashy surface.

Evans, aware that his real reason for coming to Europe is the search for that "IT" which "wants to get out," moves with difficulty and constant self-interrogation toward and beyond each of the others. In each, he discerns the pull of an unknown eros that is partly his own unreleased potential and partly a more dangerous infatuation with what he now senses himself to be. He moves rather easily past the young literary collaborator, Jack Murry, and the sleek-haired café habituée, Delise. A brief reunion with his own sister Bess (who incarnates chiefly their reserved English inheritance, in contrast to the dominance in Evans of their southern European strain) ends when she leaves Paris with a man in a somewhat desperate effort to break out of her American predicament of being "all tied up, letting the wrong things out."

Evans himself travels south with Lou Martin, gay and athletic, for whom his trip to Europe had ostensibly been planned. When on the Riviera she suddenly leaves him to marry a rich Englishman, he feels both a loss and a release. She is throwing off what he must retain: "a burden—the necessity of invention." Disconsolate but freed, he continues his course of abandonment into Italy: through the dark night in Genoa, which reveals itself to be a fruitful nothingness, the source of all making; to Florence and the Santa Croce, where he finds "an unguessed holiness" that may emerge "if we be clean"; and on to Rome and to the Venus who manifests herself again for him. After several rather daunting attempts to move farther toward the clarity of Greece—realizing that "to create is to shoot a clarity through the oppressing, obsessing murk of the world," but caught between "the stonelike reality of ancient excellence and the pulpy worthlessness of every day"—he moves northward to Vienna, to engage more directly the problem of his relation to contemporary science and art.

This engagement occurs partly at Knobloch's clinic, where he meets a "strange inhuman art of curing" quite different from "his own soft western kind," and partly through his relation to a Miss Black. She is "like no one else he had ever in his life seen before, yet he seemed always to have known her." Personifying what has been most deeply hidden in himself, she releases, through her strangely essayistic tirades, the sharpest of aristocratic attacks upon America. However, despite her verbal angularity and European fixation, her name—he discovers—is Grace; and her body is to him "faintly coppery." Behind that antithetical mask, he is encountering American and personal depths:

> In his room he seemed to be sinking back through imprisoning circles of dark light as through the center of a flower, back to some dimly remembered past, Indian games—mad escapades. Back, back to a lost grace—his own early instincts, perfect and beautiful. Scale after scale dropped from him. . . . He never felt less voluptuous, but clarified through and through, not the mind, not the spirit—but the whole body—clear, clear, clear as if he were made of some fine material strong yet permeable to every sense—opening, loosening, letting in the light.

Such a moment, however, does not solve the problem of his personal relation to Grace. He cannot remain with her in Europe; she will not return with him to America. She recognizes the hopeless coldness of her self-exile but accuses him of running away from an aristocratic fineness that he mistakenly fears. But he answers, in semi-Lawrentian fashion: "I feel a real need for the vulgar. I have been accused before of running away. Well, I want to plant it, IT; to see if it grows. Fineness, too much of it, narcotizes me. It drives me wild. I do not want that."

Having left Grace in Vienna, Evans rejoins Bess in Geneva and travels with her to Paris. On the rebound from her own European love experience, she is now ready to entrap him. This incestuous note, of course, has sounded in all the relations with figures who are really projections of Evans's own psyche. (Grace had said, "Lovers are all brothers and sisters—like you and your little Bess"; and Evans had excitedly followed the deathward course of Sigmund and Siglinda at the opera. But Bess embodies the most difficult temptation: the disguised defeatism of Evans's own rational and moral impulses. She would bind him to herself by urging a "morality" that she has discerned in French artists: "To use well what we have, that's all."

But she would, in effect, end exploration and prevent the necessary rediscovery of America. Evans refuses to remain with her as a moral artist-in-exile, but he is almost inarticulate in their final debates. At one point he says simply: "America . . . There are some things there—still some things I want to gather." Despite a lingering farewell, he breaks away from that most insidious enemy, the sister-soul who would stop his life with a moral conclusion. His intent implicitly clarified by his journey of self-discovery, his trail of spiritual incest momentarily behind him, he sails for America alone. What will emerge from his new wholeness must, in the nature of things, remain unknown. The novel ends with the sentence: "So this is the beginning."

IV. JANUARY: A NOVELETTE

The beginning, of course, is always now. That is partly what is meant by the structure of *January: A Novelette.* Although it is close to Williams's understanding of Soupault, whose *Les Dernières Nuits de Paris* he found delightful and "accurate to the rules of conversation," the *Novelette* cannot be understood merely by categorizing it as Surrealist or Dadaist. We must give full weight to Williams's own comment to Pound: "The *Novelette* contains something I have been trying for half my life" [*Selected Letters*]. It attempts to fulfill in prose the understanding of writing toward which Williams had been working in *Kora in Hell* and in *Spring and All:* it seeks to approach and realize "the moment" itself.

In a form more disjunctive and convoluted than that of *The Great American Novel,* through conversations more "actual" than those of *In the American Grain,* the *Novelette* would render the fierce singleness that occurs when the field of contact is defined by a continuing emergency: "Thus the epidemic had become a criticism—to begin with. In the seriousness of the moment—not even the seriousness but the single necessity—the extraneous dropped of its own weight." The January epidemic is both occasion and metaphor: "a stress pares off the inanity by force of speed and a sharpness, a closeness of observation, of attention come through." Then one may apprehend the simplicity of disorder: "all things enter into the singleness of the moment and the moment partakes of the diversity of all things." The result is "conversation as design." Such conversation—in contrast to "smoothed" realistic works that are "dis-jointed" because bearing "no relation to anything in the world or in the mind"—reveals the disjunctive relatedness of the actual.

The conversations of the *Novelette* itself focus mainly on the difficulties of approaching such actuality. There are ironic lapses into fatigue after a brief inventory of revelations: "No use, no use. The banality wins, is rather increased by the attempt to reduce it. Better to learn to write and to make a smooth page no matter what the incoherence of the day, no matter what erasures must be sacrificed to improve a lying appearance to keep ordered the disorder of the pageless actual." Or the moment may seem to have just passed: "Try as I will the thing comes only when I have one stocking on, the telephone is ringing, my mind is full of difficulties and you have asked me a question. In a flash it comes and is gone. Words on a par with trees." But such difficulties are themselves part of the actual and must therefore be included in the attempted design: "This is, after all, the substance, therefore, the explanation, of my poems and my life in which *there exists* (instead of 'you exist')."

But the abundance of low-pressure material and of explanation itself prevents the *Novelette* from achieving in any full sense the design of the actual. Its style exhibits incomplete awareness of the fact that every moment is a moment of crisis. The disjunctive form it contemplates, and to some extent *is*, appears more fully in the later *Paterson*. And, by a paradox that the *Novelette* itself denies, its "conversation as design" or writing "such as unrelated passing on the street" often appears most successfully in Williams's later "realistic" prose fictions. The relation between the author and his vision thus artificially smoothed, he can then seem to give his full attention to the significant disjunctions in the world about him.

However, the more basic paradox of that later "realism" is stated by the *Novelette* itself: only through indirect means may the "light" of the attention be revealed. "What can I say? Who shall describe the light? It is like an epidemic; it is like your love." That oblique revelation of light or love is the meaning of the actual in a poem:

> Would you consider a train passing—or the city in the icy sky—a
> love song? What else? It must be so.
> And if I told you the dark trees against the night sky and the row
> of the city's lights beyond and under them—would you consider *that*
> a love statement?
> This is what my poems have been from the first.

A "love song," then, is a rendering of the actual—substance and explanation of a New World, of a life in which "*there exists*."

JOSEPH N. RIDDEL

Williams and the Ek-stasy of Beginnings

*The only human value of anything, writing included, is intense vision of the
facts, add to that by saying the truth and action upon them—clear into the
machine of absurdity to a core that is covered.*
  *God—Sure if it means sense. "God" is poetic for the unobtainable.
Sense is hard to get but it can be got. Certainly that destroys "God," it
destroys everything that interferes with simple clarity of apprehension.*
                    —The Descent of Winter

*The concept of the beginning of a river is of course a symbol of all
beginnings.*
                    —I Wanted to Write a Poem

"I am a beginner," says the narrator of *The Great American Novel*; "I am an
American. A United Stateser." The sentiments recall Whitman, but the bravado
protests too much. Adam has grown testy. Williams is certainly in the "Adamic"
tradition of American poetry, as one of our major critics has called it; but he
stands at the near end, the doubly self-conscious end, of that tradition. He writes
in and of a time when, in Wallace Stevens's words, the old gods have been "an-
nihilated," leaving us "feeling dispossessed and alone in a solitude, like children
without parents." Stevens's figures are a measure of the passage of the Adamic
poet beyond "Hegelian formulas," as Whitman once called his poems; they are
the language of the poet who has doubly fallen. "A great poem is no finish to a
man or woman but rather a beginning"—thus the bard of the 1855 edition of
Leaves of Grass, who recognized like Charles Olson's Melville, though with less
shock, that "We are the last 'first' people."

From *The Inverted Bell: Modernism and the Counterpoetics of William Carlos Williams.*
© 1974 by Louisiana State University Press. Originally entitled "The Ek-stasy of
Beginnings."

It would be possible to write a "history" of American poetics in terms of "beginnings," or better, in terms of the changing sense of beginning. For as Williams concluded, *American* is synonymous with *beginner*, and a beginner is one who, if he is not to be condemned to repeat the past, is bound to reinterpret it and thus to create his own time. He is not Whitman's "literatus." The American poet, Williams suggests, is any poet committed to the endless search for his own origins. He is committed, that is, to the paradoxical role of depriving himself of all his myths in his effort to discover a primary myth—an idea coincident with things, where his new beginning will not be repetition. He is committed, therefore, to doing violence to the very thing he loves, the romance of his native history, in order to reveal the ground of his own historicity. For he is aware, ironically, that his every effort to recover his innocence, to speak the primary myth, which is the act of Adamic naming, is an act of mediation (of interpretation) which throws him once more into history. He must repeat a beginning that is already broken with the origin.

Williams's "United Stateser" is different from Whitman's "literatus," to put it another way, as the idea of play is different from the idea of presence and absence. For Williams, the poet must be a beginner because he can no longer accept the myth of presence, of meaning given from outside one's "place." American poetry and American history have been misinterpreted, Williams argues, because of the poets' and historians' embrace of tradition, their perpetuation of the myth of the Idea, whether it is the myth of Western history, of Christianity, or of Literature. Every attempt to escape the myth of presence, even Whitman's radical democratization, only reconfirmed it. The beginnings Whitman speaks of, then, disguise the myth of the Idea in the metaphors of process and continue the dominant Platonic tradition which bears within itself a self-evident plenitude of meaning. This plenitude fills language, permeates all utterance, and words become at once things themselves and a transparence of Spirit.

The continuity of American poetry, to employ Roy Harvey Pearce's appropriate metaphor, is characterized by a series of radical discontinuities. Our Adamic poets have, at every turn, had to try to begin again, to supply and resupply a succession of privileged centers as old ones were demystified and disappeared: the Puritans' wrathful God for the Anglican Word; the Deist's Reason for the Puritan God; the Transcendental Spirit for Deity; Self for Spirit; self for Self. Finally, as Wallace Stevens says, the dominant Idea became the idea of deprivation and dispossession, and the poets found themselves in the last believable center. The creative self, the "literatus," the imagination became the latest myth of the subject as presence, and when it in turn was questioned for its immanence, it proved to be "unreal": "When the time came for them to go, it was a time when their aesthetic had become invalid in the presence not of a greater aesthetic of the same kind, but of a different aesthetic." This is the moment of double self-consciousness which marks the Modern poet's Adamism from the Transcendental Adamism of Emerson or Whitman. It envisions a world with an *absence* rather than a *presence* at its center, and thus a world, or more precisely, an "aesthetic," that is different from the old. It would be something of an oversimplification to distinguish the two aesthetics as a difference between a privileged consciousness and a dislocated self-consciousness; indeed, Stevens's insistence on naming the new time an aesthetic reveals the sameness (or *like*) implied in any talk of *difference*. Absence (Stevens's "unreal" imagination) ties itself to presence (the real of reality). Stevens's poetics remains uneasily within presence/absence metaphysics.

The continuity of Adamism in American poetics is certainly the continuity of successive (not progressive) new beginnings, of having to provide a new aesthetic, to reinvent the subjective and thus to reinvent history and language *as if* at their origins. And this is true whether the poet is intent on recovering some original Word, like Hart Crane, or, like Stevens, on providing a new aesthetic which "from the point of view of greatness was that of an intenser humanity." But the most radical invention, Williams discovered, was provoked by the metaphysical deprivation that ultimately brought even the finite self into question, as Nietzsche's death of God pronounced the end of man. For that not only emptied the house of being, it dispersed the locus of history. It made the "point of departure" a fiction. In Stevens's words, this forces the "American" poet to accept the possibility that our primordial "parents" were not human after all and that the dream of an "intenser humanity" was simply the last great "fiction," the "passion for yes." It also forces him to confront the violence of origins, the terrifyingly inhuman power of the origin which we name in order to pacify.

Stevens, it is true, had played with that very possibility as inherent within his new aesthetic. The annihilation of the gods was, for him, a freeing of the self from the "old nostalgias," or beliefs, which tied the self to a parent before or beyond the world. It was at once a deprivation and a dislocation of the self, an emptying of the self to the point of nothingness. But even at that point of utter "poverty"—when as Crispin experienced it the "whole/Shebang," including man's "mythology of self," exited—absence itself had to be imagined: "The absence of the imagination had / Itself to be imagined." Stevens clung to the late Cartesian fiction, of an "increasingly human self," the fiction of the center in man, even when he admitted it was problematic: the moonlight and Aquinas "spoke, / Kept speaking, of God. I changed the word to man." Stevens's humanism, however, presumes that we "believe without belief, beyond belief": "the nicer knowledge of / Belief, that what it believes in is not true." And though his "imagination" retains vestiges of Romantic "nostalgia," the idea of a "shaping spirit," he is just as likely to place the center elsewhere, in reality, and more important, in the ultimate belief-beyond-belief in the possible marriage of idea and thing. In other words, Stevens employs every doubt except a doubt of the fictional necessity of presence. He can thus maintain a belief in the "source of perfection." The source of perfection lay in the self's capacity to think beyond itself, to be other in the presence of the Other. This allows man to live in discontinuous and successive acts of the mind (those incarnations of the self in words) and thus to perpetuate a fiction of a continuous self. The imagination could project the "giant on the horizon," the "giant of parental magnitude," as an image of man the seeker after a perfection he could never possess. In that projection, man could give himself the fiction of futurity. He could cast an image of himself, paradoxically, as potentially the "centre on the horizon." In the end, Stevens is a Modernist poet on the verge of a new beginning. He never quite escapes the ultimate Cartesian cleavage: "Adam / In Eden was the father of Descartes," and the "supreme" must therefore always be a fiction, that presence which is unimaginable except that its absence cannot be imagined. The later Stevens marks the impasse of a sophisticated Adamism, for his Adam is the father of Western history, of consciousness. His poet or "central man" is the figurative father of the problematic of language.

In that notoriously contentious prologue to *Kora in Hell*, Williams first recorded his clash with Stevens over the place, or centrality, of imagination. Responding to a letter from Stevens, in which Stevens had remarked on the unnecessarily miscellaneous character of the poems in *Al Que Quiere!*, Williams rejected what he called the "apparition" of a "finality" in nature, comparing the fiction of that belief to a belief in literature as a sacred order of its own. The argument, very briefly, turned on Stevens's insistence that a "book" should have a center, or be centered around a "fixed point of view." To "fidget with points of view," Stevens had written, "leads always to new beginnings and incessant new beginnings lead to sterility." Stevens's insistence on the idea of a "book," and hence on the superior order of poetry with its privileged and stable center (of imagination locating itself in the world) is clear enough evidence of an early romanticism about which his later work would vacillate. Williams, on the other hand, had recognized his own affinities with Imagism, and responded that his apparent randomness was in fact his belated version of " 'Vortex' after the fashion of London, 1913." Stevens's insistence on the central imagination, says Williams, creates a poetry of "associational or sentimental value" which is, indeed, "lack of imagination." The imagination, he goes on, must not subsume the "object" and compose things by an "easy lateral sliding," that is, relate things metaphorically by resemblances. On the contrary, it must bring things into "one plane," and allow for the "flexible, jagged resort. It is to loosen the attention, my attention since I occupy part of the field." The argument between Stevens and Williams comes down to something like the distinction Roman Jakobson has made between metaphor and metonymy, and thus between two reciprocal functions of language that in turn imply two very different origins. The field of metonymic art, characterized by contiguity and successivity, and by difference, reveals a center which is everywhere and nowhere, in which imagination is a force and not a focus.

It could very well be argued here that the germ of Williams's poetics is contained in this debate, but at this point it is necessary only to stress the "field" or single "plane" on which self and objects mutually coexist in an imaginative category. The self and nature are different, but they occupy the same field, and are not defined hierarchically. Indeed, self and thing are identical only in the relation of their reciprocal difference. In the imaginative category, each is a center or locus of intersecting forces. The field admits no fixed or locatable center, and thus no *a priori* subject. This is, in effect, Williams's new aesthetic which, as Stevens foresaw, would demand incessant new beginnings, Williams's very antidote to the sterility of literature. For literature, as he admonished Hilda Doolittle (H. D.) in that same prologue, had assumed a sacredness by arriving at a "point of arrest where stabilization has gone on past the time"—or, to put it simply, literature had come to repeat itself in its search for a perfect order. Literature had valorized itself, or become institutionalized, as our new fiction of presence. "There is nothing sacred about literature, it is damned from one end to the other. There is nothing in literature but change and change is mockery"—thus Williams commits himself to an imagination which will "make its way by compass and follow no path." It will follow no prescriptions of truth and beauty. It will not metaphorize or anthropomorphize nature. Modern poetry must take the way of the "wanderer," the self moving amid things on the plane of things, in a field of incessantly changing relations and hence of "incessant new beginnings." Only then will it be like ancient poetry, or better, like original poetry. But if one has memory, how can one escape history? How can one avoid the knowledge of his distance from origins, the pathos of his repeated beginnings?

II

At one of the crucial points in *Paterson*, Book Three (a poem of acute reversals) where apocalypse and revelation, beginning and end, meet and entwine in a complex of styles and thematic evocations, Dr. Paterson confronts the problematic of his utterance:

> How to begin to find a shape—to begin to begin again,
> turning the inside out: to find one phrase that will

> lie married beside another for delight . ?
> —seems beyond attainment   .

In its larger context, the passage becomes an "American" style, a glimpse of what Williams means by beginnings. In three full pages preceding this quotation, Dr. Paterson has offered: an example of "broken" style, including a surrealistic exercise in typographical violence; a "letter" from Pound offering him a reading list which includes myth, history, and anthropology as correlative studies; and a page devoted entirely to the measure of Paterson's geological substrata, as recorded at an artesian well near the Passaic Rolling Mill, a careful reminder that one's pursuit of water to the source involves a precise, scientific measure of the ground one lives on. Immediately preceding the passage cited above, Dr. Paterson repeats a phrase from Thomas Gray's churchyard "Elegy" (in the parodic visual form of an inverted pyramid, or drill) in order to suggest, possibly, the implications of a probing descent to the elemental ground, to the darkness where ends and beginnings intersect. The "Elegy" reference is followed by a broken prose stanza on the effects of the Paterson flood of 1902, from out of the "detritus" of which there appears the "attractive brokenness" of a few recovered "stones" (like the other ubiquitous "rocks" of the poem) which the poet envisions for future "garden uses."

Immediately following the question of how to find a new "shape," Dr. Paterson records George Barker's remark that "*American poetry is a very easy subject to discuss for the / simple reason that it does not exist.*" The context, however, doubles Barker's irony and defines "American" poetry with a proper tautology—it is literally the poetry of ex-istence, of coming to be or standing forth, and is to be identified only in its primordial qualities as a language which always precedes reflection. Like the attractive brokenness of the stones emerging from the "granular stench" of the flood; like the fragmentation of the surrealist montage; like the original madness of Pound, conflating Frobenius's *Paideuma* and Ovid's *Metamorphoses* as a primordial "Everyman" library of beginnings; like the layer-on-layer of sandstone (water rock) which lines the artesian well at Paterson—like all these, American poetry is a "shape" in its primordial condition, which insistently names itself as elemental. Williams would later figure this fetal "shape" as the old man on the bridge in *The Desert Music*, just as earlier he had tentatively defined the "great American novel" [see *Imaginations* (New York: New Directions, 1971)] as the emerging new form itself, altogether different from the aesthetic of the traditional (English) novel form. An "American" novel must literally precede definition. But in this same sense, of course, its consciousness of its own newness becomes a discourse on its own primordiality—a metapoetry.

"To begin to begin again"—that is "American" poetry. And thus if one insists on looking at it as "literature," as a precious object with a revealed presence and traditional value, he will see the very opposite of the traditional "work" of art, the formal product of a creative imagination. For beginning implies beginning "to find," and thus a "broken composition," as Williams called it in the prologue to *Kora in Hell*. In poetry, this implies a launching out without prescribed rules, with a compass but no marked path; in history, it is the urge to explore, to go beyond the boundaries of the named and known, a desire to know the original point where water and rock were one, where time and place were married—to know, as he puts it in *Paterson*, "the myth / that holds up the rock," the "inspiring terror" concealed in the "cavern" where the "profound cleft" first took place. These are figures of a primordial time of emergence, the moment of that "profound cleft," and the voice of the "father of all / speech." The beginning, for the American poet, is his beginning of his search for a new language, and thus for the origins of language itself. His beginning, therefore, is never at the source, but somewhere downstream from the source, or outside the cavern whence he came and where the "father" of his cleaved (historical) thought remains shrouded.

The American poet begins in a history, and thus as the recipient of a language, which he must deny or destroy or, more exactly, turn inside out if he is to "begin again." "Now I am not what I was when the word was forming to say what I am," proclaims the narrator of *The Great American Novel*. His beginning is preoccupied with the problematic of beginnings. "If there is progress then there is a novel," he begins. "Without progress there is nothing. Everything exists from the beginning. I was a slobbering infant." Ex-istence is a fall into a language which carries the "I" farther and farther from that beginning, an experience which brings the teleological idea of "progress" into doubt even as it creates the "I." The "I" does not create but is created with the fiction of progress, the fiction of the cause as Nietzsche called it. *The Great American Novel* progresses by turning the idea of progress inside out—progress away from the beginning toward an ideal end, the teleological view of progress, becomes progress inward toward origins: "Words progress into the ground"; "A novel must progress toward a word," but not toward "*the* word"; and progress is a "game," the game of liberation, of moving "with the words" to the point where the words are broken free "from the world," or received knowledge; and the self is there with them, as in a "church" which is also the "Wife," everything co-existing in the "dreams of his babyhood." Progress is backward and inward, the "movement" of words or of "writing" which breaks up the novel's "fixed form" in its pursuit of what the Dadaist's called *rien*, the place of the origin of things. But each step of this progress, this deconstruction of successive ideas of the center, only produces another figure for origins, each pointing further back to the point of birth, that original violence. The novel progresses by violence, the play of interpretations over other interpretations.

"So this is the beginning." Thus the end of *A Voyage to Pagany* announces the novel's journey, and also the novel, as a pretext. The new beginning follows Dr. Evans's return from a search for the "point of his departure, the place of his birth." The place is Rome, where pagan and Christian history converge. Rome is the origin of the myth of history, the city which barely suppresses the pagan roots which would bring into question the teleological myth of the West. Rome also is imitation Greece, but it has suppressed the pagan vitality of classicism. Evans's trip to Vienna, where he studies pediatrics but more significantly strikes up an affair with some mysterious dark lady and begins to write, provides the clue to the meaning of the voyage. There, he discovers himself to be an obstetrician of the "word." The most obvious implication of his brief affair, and his studies in this Freudian center, is its release of his own suppressed energy, the beginning of his birth as a writer-discoverer that leads inevitably toward the novel's end and his beginning. What Evans seeks to recover at his "place of birth" is the buried "gods." The "death of the gods," and therefore the beginning of Western history, has impoverished Europe he discovers: the Europeans "starve, not because there is no food but because there is no one to give it to them any more." His search for his sources, for the old dead gods, is the manifestation of his desire for a "burning presence under the veneer of to-day." In his feverish writing, "he had penetrated too far the veil of dust the gods had thrown up about their secrets to protect them," and therefore, "Panting with desire to possess" the secret, "he feels it slipping away nevertheless and calls it, strives to call it by a name, strives to fasten it in his sight—real among its everyday disguises." Writing pursues a "secret" endlessly, and possesses only what slips away or what it destroys: he "liked the unknown best . . . a presence nearer than the nearest day he had ever known."

In *An Introduction to Metaphysics*, Martin Heidegger records the history of what he calls the original misinterpretation in metaphysics, the cleavage which took place in the Socratic interpretation of the pre-Socratics, the original error of separating words from things, meaning from being, or, in the original Greek terms, *logos* from *physis*. It is a sophisticated and complex argument, but the gist of it can be summarized as follows: that the history of philosophy is the history of thought separating itself from being, so that we can no longer stand in the presence of being as that which is disclosed or unconcealed. Therefore, we no longer understand the reciprocal difference between *logos* and *physis*, thinking and being, as it existed, for example, at the beginning of philosophical thinking, figuratively in the pre-Socratics. For *logos* and *physis*, he argues, were originally words which incorporated in themselves "being," in the sense of that which comes into being—is disclosed, or unconcealed (*aletheia*)—in the sense of opening out from some hypothetical origin. In the rational breaking apart of the two words, the original sense of this emerging power was lost to both, *physis* being reduced to something like physics or nature and *logos*, to idea or reason. The cleavage of rational thinking has led to an obscuring of the reciprocal difference of *physis* and *logos*. The inextricability of being as that which emerges or breaks out or stands up (*physis*) and of being as that which is gathered together or collected (*logos*) changes into the priority of *logos* or reason to *physis* or things. It must be the effort of original thinking, says Heidegger, to return to original thinking, and thus to repeat itself. But this does not mean to take received thoughts and apply them to the world. To repeat original thinking is to return, in the act of thought, to the original unfolding, or unconcealment, to the experience of "origin as emergence." This thinking reveals to us not that "thinking and being are the same," as the Parmenidean maxim has historically been interpreted (subordinating being to the *a priori* of the *logos*) but that thinking *and* being are reciprocally interrelated as primordial opposites, and thus the irreducible pairs of all beginnings.

Heidegger demands a new beginning to our thinking man's historical adventure: "But we do not repeat a beginning by reducing it to something past and now known, which need merely be imitated; no, the beginning must be begun again, more radically, with all the strangeness, darkness, insecurity that attend a true beginning." Man's power is language; man is the creature who realizes his humanness by being projected into the *place* of his speech. Thus poetry is, for Heidegger, language involved in its original work—the disclosure of being. But it is always involved in the crisis of beginnings. "Unconcealment," the original coming into being, is a beginning which man is repeatedly losing:

> Since it is a beginning, the beginning must in a sense leave itself behind. (Thus it necessarily conceals itself, but this self-concealment is not nothing.) A beginning can never directly preserve its full momentum; the only possible way to preserve its force is to repeat, to draw once again . . . more deeply than ever from its source. And it is only by repetitive thinking . . . that we can deal appropriately with the beginning and the breakdown of truth. The need (Not) of being and the greatness of its beginning are no object of a merely historical observation, explanation, and evaluation. This does not preclude but rather requires that the historical course of this collapse be as far as possible elucidated.

Thus we return to "unconcealment" through "work"—"the work of the word in poetry, the work of stone in temple and statue, the work of word in thought."

Poetry and philosophy become original poetry and philosophy not by extending received truths but by repeating the original act of unconcealment, which involves a breaking up (deconstruction) of the already unconcealed, those received historical forms.

Heidegger offers a number of entrances into Williams's poetics. For as Heidegger knew, the search of the philosopher (especially the modern philosopher of "deconstruction") and of the naïve poet is a common search, though they occupy, in the phrase of Hölderlin held so dear by Heidegger, dwellings on the "peaks of time" which are "near to one another, / Tired on mountains farthest apart." Williams's intuition that, at the origin, there are "no ideas but in things," his sense of modern man "blocked" from his sources, his awareness that the "language has failed" man by divorcing him from the power of his beginnings— these reveal the common *ground* the post-Modern poet and the "deconstructive" philosopher must seek. The poet is aware that he "begins" historically somewhere apart from his sources, and thus within the received language and values of history, so that his beginning is a search for beginnings. Yet, it is a beginning which like all beginnings launches him out from the unknown into the unknown. It is an act which involves him in "all the strangeness, darkness, insecurity that attend a true beginning."

If beginnings are necessarily concealed, left behind, they are, as Heidegger says, "not nothing," since they are everything that being is "Not." The seeker after beginnings is a seeker after his necessarily concealed sources who, like the poet breaking down language in search of its concealed primordiality, acts out his role at a point nearer the source than other men. Thus Heidegger's figure of the *site* of poetry. The poet acts in a "place" (*topos*) that is neither a total unity (the place of the gods) nor totally within history (like the place of the common man, who is spoken by his language, that "idle talk" which constitutes the "they"). The poet *places* himself at the point of e-mergence, of disclosure, of the coming to light of being. He is an in-between man. The significance of Williams's poetics lies in the rediscovery of the poet's *place* in history—not as an individual talent who stands at the present point some distance from the source of his continuous tradition, but as one standing in the proximity of his source, and thus in the proximity of history's beginning. Williams's poetics echoes Heidegger's in insisting that the role of the poet is to participate in the act of "inaugural naming"; therefore, his *place* is the place where language breaks out, where we are brought into the presence of its first appearing, its beginning to take "shape," its flowering.

Williams's first significant poem, "The Wanderer," is an adventure of the poet taking his "place," of his ADVENT. The young "novitiate" of "The Wanderer" has his advent in a question put to him by his muse-crone, an old woman in the form of a "young crow" who compels him to seek a new place and role: "How shall I be a mirror to this modernity?" The question is accompanied by her own natural metamorphoses, her final form being that of a "great sea-gull" who vanishes with a "wild cry": and "in my mind all the persons of godhead / Followed after." The vanishing of the "godhead" leaves him alone, at one with her in "whom age in age is united," attendant upon the "first day of wonders." He comes to occupy, with her, a place of original difference, "out of sequence." It is a place without perspective, without past or future, with one "face." The young poet is brought into the presence of "the first day," a day of the primordial "Taking shape" of a "high wanderer." He becomes a part of, not apart from, nature as change.

Awkward and tentative though it is, "The Wanderer" struggles to articulate the perspectiveless moment of human beginnings, the simultaneous beautiful terror of life emerging from the immediacy of a "gutter," of life coming to definition as culture out of nature, or language out of the simultaneity of things and forms. He pleads to be "lifted still, up and out of terror, / Up from before the death living before me." His initiation, then, is an introduction to the necessity of taking his place as wanderer, in the midst of the river's "rottenness." The river is a place of simultaneous ends and beginnings, where a chaos of potential forms broils about him, without "sequence." His "ecstasy" (literally, his ek-stasy) ended, his "life" begins. It is a "new wandering." His leap into the "filthy Passaic" is a baptism, a sinking in, a resignation to nature, a return to the "crystal beginning of its days." But at that place, the river "rebound[s]" and leaps forward. The melting of sense and sense, of subject and object, is a point of "rebound," the renewal of the eternal movement "backward and forward," a reversal. It is also an e-mergence, the beginning of the new difference of subject and object. He has moved from place to act (ecstasy—ek-stasy). Poet and river are not married in a primal unity, or stasis, but in terms of a primordial or original opposition. The poet, the subject, is born a wanderer: not an essential or pure self, detached from the world, or a soul with transcendent origins; nor, especially, is he a subject lost in the primacy of the other. The wanderer takes his identity, as poet, only in his immediate and reciprocal relation with the river. He is situated. The relation is the essential opposition and reciprocity of thinking and being. The "wanderer" is the language of the river, admonished by the old woman to "Be mostly silent." Time is "washed finally under," and a new time begins in the river's "rebound." The "new wandering" of the young poet is (to be) the on-going speech of the place, which is "mostly silent." It is a new speech emerging from the reversal of the old, a turning of the inside out. Wandering, quite simply, is the condition of original cleavage. The wanderer is original man. He is historical man, a Cain figure, an ecstatic condemned to repeated new beginnings.

In his *Novelette*, Williams's narrator speaks of the beginning of life in terms very similar to the young wanderer's beginning, not as a "progress upward" but a "progress downward to the beast. To the actual. To the devil with silks. But there cannot be an objection to an intelligent cutting away of obscurity that is not a return to an old cesspool. Violent nonsense." This progress, like that of *The Great American Novel* and *Kora in Hell*, involves a violence and a sinking of sense into sense, a descent into "nonsense." It enacts the necessary closing of Cartesian distance that Hillis Miller finds to be the starting point of Williams's poetics.

Years afterward, Williams described the experience which motivated "The Wanderer" as his "resignation to existence," a "sort of nameless religious experience" which wiped out the distancing, sequential order of time and reconciled him with his present world and thus with the "first day of wonders": it was "a despair which made everything a unit and at the same time a part of myself. . . . Where shall one go? What shall one do? Things have no names for me and places no significance. As a reward for this anonymity I feel as much a part of things as trees and stones. Heaven seems frankly impossible. I am damned as I succeed. I have no particular hope save to repair, to rescue, to complete." His confession illuminates the condition of "new wandering," for the wanderer is one deprived of all hope of self-transcendence, or even of an identity apart from place, of a self apart from the field it walks, and takes intimate measure of, or designs. But the wanderer is not merely an object among objects; he is a language, a completer or rescuer. Williams's "resignation to existence," like the young poet's leap into the "filthy Passaic," is in two senses a "nameless religious experience": it is the assumption of anonymity and a reciprocal placing of the subject in the field of a mutually defined and defining other. It is literally a re-sign-ation, or the beginning of a new act of naming. "To repair, to rescue, to complete"—the poet as namer does complete by re-signing his place, and his new naming is intrinsic to the simultaneous coming into being of himself and his place. It is a place not so much defined as in process of definition, of being named.

The artist Edward Dahlberg once reminded Williams in a letter which is included in Book One of *Paterson*, is an Ishmael whose wandering incorporates the "affliction" of restlessness, of desire. But the name of the original wanderer is Cain, the exiled and violent "son"—the son of the original namer. The archetypal wanderer exists in the land of Nod (of dream), a murderer and man marked for murder. He is a man resigned to existence, and thus man who willfully murders the unobtainable "God" for the obtainable "sense," the "simple clarity of apprehension," as Williams calls it. He is a man unwilling to accept the old names of his father, one hungry to pursue sense to the concealed "core" of being. He is a man whose freedom is reciprocal with his mortality, who exists in "action." The wanderer is one who takes his place somewhere beyond the concealed and silent origin of history but refuses to be dominated by history. He is not quite at "home"—and thus, like Cain, wanders in the land of dream—but neither is he entirely of the people. He is restless for some new ground, some city. The wanderer is a builder of cities. . . .

The poet, as Heidegger says in his remarkable essays on Hölderlin, stands somewhere between the gods and the people, and thus is an outcast, an in-between man who stands closest to the unnameable, mysterious power of origins. It is only through him—his naming of the gods or mediation of their otherwise silent signs and the common voice (idle talk) of the people—that we can come to understand the true nature of man as the coming into being of language. For in the end, Williams gives a role to the poet, outcast and anonymous, that recalls Heidegger's paradoxical view of the poet whose original utterance is also a poetry about poetry:

> Hölderlin writes poetry about the essence of poetry—but not in the sense of a timelessly valid concept. This essence of poetry belongs to a determined time. But not in such a way that it conforms to this time, as to one which is already in existence. It is that Hölderlin, in the act of establishing the essence of poetry, first determines a new time. It is the time of the gods that have fled *and* of the god that is coming. It is the time of *need*, because it lies under a double lack and a double Not: the No-more of the gods that have fled and the Not-yet of the god that is coming.

III

In one of the improvisations of *Kora in Hell*, Williams muses on the fate of the old gods and the situation (the site) of the Modern poem:

> Giants in the dirt. The gods, the Greek gods, smothered in filth and ignorance. The race is scattered over the world. Where is its home? Find it if you've the genius. Here Hebe with a sick jaw and a cruel husband,—her mother left no place for a brain to grow. Herakles rowing boats on Berry's Creek! Zeus is a country doctor without a taste for coin jingling. Supper is of a bastard nectar on rare nights for they will come—the rare nights! The ground lifts and out sally the heroes of Sophokles, of Æschylus. They go seeping down into our hearts, they rain upon us and in the bog they sink again down through

the white roots, down. . . . It's all of the gods, there's nothing else
worth writing of. They are the same men they always were—but
fallen. Do they dance now, they that danced beside Helicon? They
dance much as they did then, only, few have an eye for it, through
the dirt and fumes.

If all writing is of the gods, it is not of the old departed gods but of their eternal
power to return. The gods anticipated by the Modern poet are "fallen gods," or
gods scattered through the single plane of the earth. That is, the present gods,
which all writing is about, are not transcendent; and because they are not, writing
emerges from a different place—any "local." Imaginative writing may be an
attempt to recover presence; but self-consciousness, its own historicity, leads it to
question its own constitutive act. It becomes in turn a questioning of the ground.
The traditional place of art is turned inside out, or is brought to the "ground."
The presence of the modern gods is not locatable in some transcendent site; their
power is suffused throughout the earth. They are fallen in the sense of scattered,
like the languages of Babel.

In the prose of *Spring and All*, Williams explores this "fall" in terms of the
new imaginative plane of cubist art. Modern art, he says, takes "familiar, simple
things" and, while maintaining their independent reality (difference), arranges
them contiguously to compose a new space. The individual things are distinct,
mimetic of the "real," but the new relation is imaginative, as in a painting by
Juan Gris in which things as logically unrelated as a "shutter, a bunch of grapes,
a sheet of music, a picture of sea and mountains" are related in a "unity" of
"admirable simplicity and excellent design." It is a picture (even a picture within
the picture) which calls attention to itself as art, as imaginative. Or as dream.
This assertion of its "detached" plane, says Williams, was "not necessary where
the subject of art was not 'reality' but related to the 'gods'—by force or otherwise. There was no need of the 'illusion' in such a case since there was none
possible where a picture or a work represented simply the imaginative reality
which existed in the mind of the onlooker. No special effort was necessary to
cleave where the cleavage already existed."

Classical art recognized the cleavage of ideal and real in taking the gods for
its subject and denying the illusion of realistic space, but the new art "cleaves"
and asserts its cleavage. Classical art could assume the presence of the gods, and
could represent their reality as an Idea. Thus it represented the constitutive power
of the Idea. "The only realism in art is of the imagination," Williams asserts, not
because art uses real things but because it "detaches" things from the ordinary
and de-signs them on a new plane. The realism of cubist synthetic art is classical
realism turned inside out, undoing the "beautiful illusion" of perspectivism.

Juxtaposition, not perspective, is the order of relation; particularity and differ-ence, not an expected syntax of relations—this defines the "field" lifted out of the ordinary. Modern art must retain the illusion of the ordinary and thus the presence of the cleavage, whereas the old art assumed the cleavage between the world and the ideal, with their respectively ambiguous and pure centers. The old art, in a sense, was at "home" in the ideal; it was a symbolic art, yet mimetic. The new reveals the artist as wanderer, in that plane between the gods and the ordinary, where "age in age is united" and "out of sequence." The old art could re-present (in Williams's terms, copy) the idea of the gods and thus was meta-phorical; the new must present (in Williams's terms, imitate) the flowering of the new gods, and thus be metonymical. The "new" therefore brings the idea of Art into question.

The new presents, however, what Heidegger calls the "new time," of the "double-Not." This new time is the time of e-mergence and, consequently, of the creative moment itself. It is a "double lack" because it reveals neither the classical decorums of hierarchical forms nor the undifferentiated chaos of immedi-ate sensations. This "time" becomes a field of distinct yet logically unrelated but contiguous things. It is decentered. As Heidegger said of Hölderlin, this kind of poet writes a "poetry about the essence of poetry," not in the sense of a para-digm to be repeated but in the sense of what Williams calls a "force moving." Thus the poetry exists at the place of cleavage, including, as *Spring and All* demonstrates, the cleavage between prose and poetry: the "jump from prose to the process of imagination is the next great leap of the intelligence." Writing "separates" words from their referent. Inevitably, this cut demands an art that is self-reflexive. This art becomes an incessant commentary on itself, calling atten-tion to its process of removing itself inwardly (plane by plane) from the ordinary: "The study of human activity is the delineation of the cresence and ebb of this force, shifting from class to class and location to location—rhythm: the wave rhythm of Shakespeare watching clowns and kings sliding into nothing." The imaginative process accentuates its artifices, the removal of things from their expected, perspectival, symbolic place.

To participate in this force, then, the poet must necessarily write a poetry that is at once doubly self-conscious and naïve, sophisticated and primitive. He willfully attacks the old forms and celebrates the primordial emergence of some new, embryonic ones which were spectrally there all along. Therefore, he must be his own critic, as the poet of *Spring and All* recognized: "whatever of dull you find among my work, put it down to criticism, not to poetry. You will not be mistaken—Who am I but my own critic? Surely in isolation one becomes a god —At least one becomes something of everything, which is not wholly godlike, yet a little so—in many things." This leads to a poetry not simply of self-exploration or prophecy, but to a poetry of self-questioning. It breaks up the illusions of perspectivism by a persistent questioning of the surface, by penetrating to the creative force "at work" in the *work*. It reveals that the force of "great works of the imagination . . . stand[s] between man and nature as saints once stood between men and sky." The poet of *Paterson*, both implicitly and explicitly, recognizes the poet's double lack, his desire which places him somewhere between the silence of the gods and the roar of the everyday language.

Paterson, in fact, begins with the death of the old gods, and the double negation of desire and fall. In an early manuscript version of Book One, Williams experimented with a dialogue between the split halves of the poetic self. He called the two voices Willie and Doc, the first a patient of the second. The Doc drinks to excess, and thinks Willie "reads too much." The Doc is obsessed with the history of the place and reads to Willie out of his numerous volumes of local New Jersey history. But Willie hardly ever reads, because he is an "agent" of the "word," the "eternal word." Before it was abandoned, the dialogue went through several alternative versions. What Williams apparently was trying to relate was the place of the poet, the site of his dream, the poet being an agent of the word and thus a deliverer of the word into history. Willie (and the colloquial name may very well intend a pun on *Wille*) has no interest in the Doc's texts, for he is an agent of the vanished origins of those texts. The Doc drinks to escape the question those texts pose, or the answers they will not disclose. The language of Willie and the Doc is the language, respectively, of poetry and prose, of the gods and of man. And the poet must uncover the ground that connects the two, like poetry and prose so apparently irreconcilable—the ground of the double-Not.

The experimental dialogue reveals Williams's concern with the Modern poet's radical self-consciousness, and discloses that his willed dream of recovering a lost presence is the result of a need to fill a lack or an absence. Later, he will discover the meaning of silence as the place of the gods. Whether to be agent of the eternal word, and thus a son of the gods, or the anonymous physician, resigned to his existence and thus no more than a rescuer or completer—this is the divided self, the self as desire, or lack, who is left to contemplate the other as his negative. This self becomes, in the poem's finished version, the figure of the poet as Dr. Paterson, who speaks and is the language of his place. But he speaks simultaneously two languages, like the poet of *Kora in Hell* who distinguishes between the traditional and contemporary poet in terms of the latter's need to conceal his artifice:

> *That which is heard from the lips of those to whom we are talking in our day's-affairs mingles with what we see in the streets and everywhere about us as it mingles also with our imaginations. By*

this chemistry is fabricated a language of the day which shifts and reveals its meaning as clouds shift and turn in the sky and sometimes send down rain or snow or hail. This is the language to which few ears are tuned so that it is said by poets that few men are ever in their full senses since they have no way to use their imaginations. Thus to say that a man has no imagination is to say nearly that he is blind or deaf. But of old poets would translate this hidden language into a kind of replica of the speech of the world with certain distinctions of rhyme and meter to show that it was not really that speech. Nowadays the elements of that language are set down as heard and the imagination of the listener and of the poet are left free to mingle in the dance.

The talk of "our day's affairs" (in *Paterson,* the "roar" of the "great beast") is language divorced from its origins, the language not of the "full senses" but of one limited separate sense. It is idle talk. The "hidden language" is a language of "full" sense. It is the language of emerging forms, of shape-shifting, of which everyday language is a sterile, secondary mediation, the residue of exhausted names. The poet's role, clearly enough, is to restore to man the sense of vital mediations, to define man as agent of the eternal word or, in other words, as the interpreter. The traditional poet moved to accommodate the world, yet sustain the illusion of poetry as a mirror not of "our day's affairs" but a transparency of some more sacred power. But the Modern poet is concerned with the reality of relations and with the elemental structures which define man at the point of his beginning, as he departs from the gods into history. The Modern poet, then, reveals the original discontinuity of this departure, of his interpretation. The "dance" . . . is the field of man's originally free relations. It is the figure of his ritual departure from nature, yet his ritual participation (and reciprocal involvement) in primary being. The Modern poet is a "wanderer," whose "place" is where nature and culture are revealed in their original interdependence and discontinuity. His "place" is language, the site of utterance, where is disclosed the original discontinuity between the gods (our names for which are only the signs of their power we no longer possess) and man. It is the place of new naming, and hence of violence or the primal murder.

The poet as wanderer, then, participates in the experience of original dislocation which Geoffrey Hartman has brilliantly described as the Romantic resistance to self-consciousness and its need to return to mythic thinking. For as Hartman says, the Romantic "journey," the primary Romantic myth, involves the fall into self-consciousness (thus solipsism) and the resulting effort (the creative act) to effect a transition from self-consciousness to imagination; the state of imagination, Hartman goes on, is in effect a return to (or desire for) the original innocence of the state of nature. It is a desire which bears within itself the impossibility of being satisfied. The source of power is inaccessible, except as this source is evoked in the sacred space (a mediation) of art, in which consciousness and nature are sustained in a timeless discontinuity. The return is possible, that is, only in the doubly stressed artifice of art. The Romantic journey repeatedly calls attention to itself as prelude or pre-text, asserts its separateness, as Williams says, or becomes a poetry about poetry. As indicated earlier, Hartman likens the Romantic myth with the myth of Orpheus, the poet doomed to failure in his desire to retrieve the sources of his own power. This myth is a significant contrast to the myth of Persephone, the myth of the cyclic continuity of nature and culture. Orpheus's legend is the legend of discontinuity, of poetry as mediation. But the post-Romantic poem—that is, the post-Modern poem—returns to both to demythologize its desire for an origin that art itself has fabricated.

The poet as wanderer incorporates both the experience of discontinuity and the dream of continuity. Descent and ascent replace either the dream of the "eternal return" (Persephone) or the tragedy of loss (Orpheus). And though Williams plays repeated variations on the Kore legend (as in *Kora in Hell*), he emphasizes the rhythm between two irreconcilable poles rather than the eternal return. Descent and ascent become endless and reciprocal acts of the poet, which generate in their reciprocity a "dance" of "contending forces," a "picture of perfect rest" like the image of the vortex. The picture is the poem which aspires to reveal itself not as perfection, or totalization, but as the "stability" of "contending forces." It is a structure of necessary opposites which denies the possibility of a superintending or transcendent source. But it is a "picture" of "perfect rest," calling attention to itself as fictional, imaginary—as art rather than nature. This distinction is crucial for Williams, because it saves him (or his poet) from the ultimate Orphic tragedy—the exhaustion of imaginative energy in the failed quest to restore or renew itself at the source, the dilemma, for example, of Hart Crane. The poet who has "resigned" himself can escape the ultimate tragedy of Orphic loss, of inevitably looking back at his own inevitable loss of presence. The self-consciousness of the Romantic poet is doubled, and therefore transformed into a resistance.

It is, perhaps, in the spirit of this recognition that Williams began an early draft of *Paterson*, Book One, with an excursus on the nature of the modern gods. "The gods should be without morals," he wrote in some early tentative lines for "The Delineaments of the Giants," because "for them there's no one upstairs. . . . They have no one else to talk to but us, gives them a sense of humor." And elsewhere he speculated on the consequence of their immorality (that is, lack of limitation): "This makes them unreal to us and dangerous. We have no counterparts to their absolutes." But it was a false start. The old gods are dead; the new ones, fallen. When Williams begins Book One of *Paterson* with "The Delineaments of the Giants," he begins with the fragments of the history of place, the exhausted *topoi* of a "time" which has lost its gods, and to which new gods have not come, because "no poet has come." He must take a "common language" and "unravel" its complex. He cannot proceed, however, as one who speaks with the absolute authority of the gods, but only as one speaking from his own tenuous place of mediation, his desire. When the poet of *Paterson*, Book Five, declares, at the beginning of March and the reawakening of his memory, that his poem is "Not prophecy! NOT prophecy! / but the thing itself!" he repeats the condition under which the entire poem functions—that the poet can no longer speak the word pure, or reveal what is outside of speech through speech. He can neither speak of what precedes speech, nor reveal a future outside the concreteness of his immediate utterance. He cannot, that is, speak symbolically or metaphorically.

The thing itself, he reveals, can only be the primary myth of original mediation itself. This myth, like the various marriage ceremonies appealed to in Book Five of *Paterson*, maintains the paradox of the sacred or pure which is necessarily violated in its fall into being. The legend of the virgin and the whore, which is the thematic center of Book Five, is the figure of the poet's act of naming. Williams's "thing itself" is not the philosopher's abstraction for essence or substance, what Nietzsche calls man's "will to power," any more than it is the cry of positivism or of the empirical object. It is his word for the poem as dance or as city, as the space of a gathering which has no origin outside itself and no fixed center within. The poem speaks the "myth / that holds up the rock," and thus speaks of what can never be unconcealed, the "secret" of the origin. The poem is an image of the "profound cleft" of the rock, where the "shrouded" figure of "Earth, the chatterer, father of all / speech" stands. The thing itself, therefore, is the form of the myth of myths, of the disclosure of *presence* as fiction. It is at once the secretion (the trace) of presence and a questioning of the "secret." The poem, like thought, is the trace of a lost origin, an image of original cleavage.

In *Paterson*, however, it is the "giants," not the gods, who are delineated, or who come to stand in the place of the old *topoi*, the giants who are the traditional mythic enemies of the gods, figures of rebellion loosed by man's original fall. The giants are figures of man's desire, challenging the gods; but in the same sense they are figural marks of the discontinuity between man and the gods. The giants of *Paterson*, Book One, embody the paradox of man's Modern (post-Romantic, and thus self-self-conscious) adventure in history. The giants can be delineated, since they are the shapes of man's emergence; that is, they are the

origin and end of man, rebels against the origin, and thus the origin and end
of language:

> We sit and talk and the
> silence speaks of the giants
> who have died in the past and have
> returned to those scenes unsatisfied
> and who is not unsatisfied, the
> silent, Singac the rock-shoulder
> emerging from the rocks—and the giants
> live again in your silence and
> unacknowledged desire—

Here, midway in the poem's first book, the poet "places" himself, and
historical man, in the paradoxical condition of his desire—as one who suffers
from the problematic of language and therefore endures Paterson's history. Yet,
he is committed to renewing himself and thus to renewing the language. He is
both Willie and the Doc of the abortive dialogue, both agent and echo of the
word. The passage quoted above locates the problem at the level of language,
which turns out to be the ground of being, of man's historicity. The giants of
Paterson are man and woman, city and park, divided by the river and therefore
no longer sustained by the source:

> A man like a city and a woman like a flower
> —who are in love. Two women. Three women.
> Innumerable women, each like a flower.

"But / only one man—like a city." That is, man is place (or *topos*), a gathering;
woman is flowering or emerging, the form of original energy. Woman is nature
and man, culture. And language is both—the language of everyday, and the
language which is "hidden." The "divorce" of Paterson is the divorce of the two,
a cleavage which conceals the original reciprocal marriage of opposites: of ideas
and things; man and woman; culture and nature; form and power. The first
book of *Paterson* is engaged in no less a primordial adventure than Heidegger's
visionary poet, Hölderlin, who provides the philosopher with his paradigmatic
line: "Much man has learnt. / Many of the heavenly ones he has named, / *Since
we have been a conversation* / And have been able to hear from one another"
(italics mine).

As Heidegger makes emphatic, these lines define man not simply as the
creation of language, but as the fallen self that is but half of any conversation;
and, more important, its past tense records his historical departure from his origins. *Since* we have been a conversation, the gods have been given names, have

become fixed as the center or presence which defines our being as a negation. But the pastness of the tense records our own departure from that inaugural act of naming, and we come to exist in a conversation that conceals the original relation. *Paterson*'s "talk" of the "giants" records the poet's awareness that, for man at the end of history, conversation must be renewed, as if at the beginning. Every poem is a renewal of the conversation, a talk which brings a "we" to-gether over the silence of their "desire." The giants, the primordial emerging rebellious energy itself, live only in the talk that marries opposites into a "we," the implied sameness and difference of coexistence. Quite simply, the giants live again only in the "thing itself" of the poem, as supplements of the origin, the silence or space of original opposition. The remarkable series of passages which surround this central naming in *Paterson*, Book One, indicates luminously that the "silence" in which the giants "live" again is the zero-degree of speech itself. The "talk" is like "air lying over water" which "lifts" (a favorite Williams word for bringing to expression or making to stand up) "the ripples, brother / to brother, touching as the mind touches, / counter-current." It marries the classical oppositions of subject and object, power and form, into a structurally reciprocal opposition: "one that whirls / backward at the brink and curls invisibly / upward," the forces which make us think "separate / worlds," or of culture as superior and separate from nature. In their "counter-current," the opposing worlds affirm "desire" as the name of man and thus as the name of language that must be at once transitive (and hence mediational) and stable (structural). The poet is forced to name language as the essentially mediatory power, and thus to name his own discontinuity with the gods. Yet he must reclaim the vitality of the giants as the name of his own desire.

Paterson, then, begins both in dream and in divorce—and the language of Paterson, whether of the place or the poet of the place, is the language of history, "forked by preconception." That is, it is either the language of fixed and recorded events which nostalgically recalls a lost and undiscoverable origin, or the nightmarish "roar" or "thunder / of the waters," a torrent of undifferentiated fluxing detail that confounds the certainty (and the silence) of its source. Divorced from the source, the people of the place are divorced from themselves (mind and body) and from each other; and since Paterson's language is simultaneously the prose of everyday and the primordial "hidden language" of poetry, it reveals the paradox of man's historicity, of his desire for and his distance from his origins:

> Immortal he neither moves nor rouses and is seldom
> seen, though he breathes and the subtleties of his machinations
> drawing their substance from the noise of the pouring river
> animate a thousand automatons. Who because they

neither know their sources nor the sills of their
disappointments walk outside their bodies aimlessly for the most
        part,
    locked and forgot in their desires—unroused.

Dr. Paterson is "immortal" because he is language and incarnates its problematic: he "lies" at the base of "spent" water (the "Falls," in fact), and thus at
the point of maximum energy turning into exhaustion (fallen, divorced, separated
out from the origin). His breath is the mystery of water itself, the primal and the
renewing element, language. His machinations are embodied in "the noise of the
pouring river," at first as the indiscriminate fluxion of vague shapes. What is
happening here is the happening of language, the original coming into being of
being, an original fall or inflection. It is a fall not from the source into separateness, however, but from its originating power into the state of auto-mata, stability. The "automatons" of Paterson are "locked" in their "desires" and do not
realize themselves in their fallenness as dependent on their "conversation"—or,
on the other, on language. Having fallen into history, they have failed to realize
their true historicity: they are the language, the "common language," indifferent.
They are "locked" in their separate "desires" (plural), or their nonidentity, and
thus cannot act (are "blocked") in terms of their true historicity. Or as Williams
put it in a later poem:

> Innocence! Innocence is the condition of heaven.
> Only in that which we do not yet know shall we
> be fêted, fed. That is to say, with ceremony. The
> unknown is our refuge toward which we hurtle
>
>   .   .   .   .
>
>   Flight
> means only desire and desire the end of flight
> stabbing there with the barbed tongue which *succeeds!*

The ceremony, the poem, is an act which feeds the lack; it is the action
between source and success, between beginning and end, the language of becoming (desire) as emerging into being, and the action of language (itself a lack)
seeking its return to the source. Ceremony is conversation—but it is a relation
recognized at the level of ritual as a fiction. The barbed tongue does succeed, for it
is speech which breaks up the ceremony of innocence and launches the action (the
succession of words in speech) toward the end of desire. It was not a naïve poet,
seeking a way out of language into innocence, who insisted in the Author's Introduction to the *The Wedge* (the title itself being a concealed pun on the "barbed
tongue" of lang-wedge) that frustration, action, and poetry were indivisible:

It is an error attributable to the Freudian concept of the thing, that the arts are a resort from frustration, a misconception still entertained in many minds.

They speak as though action itself in all its phases were not compatible with frustration. All action the same.... Who isn't frustrated and does not prove it by his actions—if you want to say so?

But through art the psychologically maimed may become the most distinguished man of his age. Take Freud for instance.

The making of poetry is no more an evidence of frustration than is the work of Henry Kaiser or Timoshenko. It's the war, the driving forward of desire to a complex end.

There are two kinds of action recorded in Book One of *Paterson*, and both are the result of desire: the action of history as violence, which leads either to a destruction of the other (of nature by civilization or natural man, the Indian, by civilized man) or of the self by itself (Sarah Cumming's swoon and fall, or Sam Patch's erratic drive, both presented as failures of communication which lead to the actors' deaths and return to a silent union with nature). Patch, of course, is the embodiment of Paterson as language, not only because his acting name is Noah Faitoute Paterson (with all the multiple implications of the biblical Noah and the American language maker), but because his act, of bridging chasms by the precarious walk on a tightrope (of overcoming the discontinuity of origin and being) confronts in its every gesture the fundamental tensions between motion and form. The arc of his first leap reveals the wonder of man's being-toward-death, his authentic launching out. That Patch's last walk takes place over the Genesee Falls under the conditions of a staged performance, an artifice which pretends to be a "wonder," reveals the condition of language separated from action. And that action is itself a departure. The attempt to rebridge clarifies original cleavage.

Patch's last act is no longer original interpretation. It is divorced from the original need of his original launching out. It therefore denies the primordial madness of his first leap, his thrust into the mystery of his futurity. His last leap is only a staged repetition. He has turned life into art and death. Idea precedes action. In Patch's first leap, "he spoke as he jumped"; in his last, speech preceded act. "What could he say that he must leap so desperately to complete it?" The first is a spontaneous leap that fulfills man's need to begin again. This leap becomes Patch's "starting point" as a performer, the great Jersey "patriot," Noah Paterson. His final leap, ironically, is an exploitation of a culture's hunger for wonder, or revelation, and leads to a "great silence." The first act is an act of original interpretation and reveals the wonder of the original fall-leap itself. It reveals death to be intrinsic to man's desire for wholeness, the doubling of his original fall. The repetitions, made for profit and not in the search for genesis, falsely reveal death as a silence outside the act, the illusory origin. Thus, his last speech reverses his act and returns him to nature, to the state of indifference.

In the case of Mrs. Cumming, her fall (leap? swoon?) is the ironic consequence of her husband's insistence that the two "set our face homeward." Home is the place of wholeness, a marriage, a place named only as that from which they have departed. Their failure of communication (sexual, social, religious) provides them no distance from the mysterious center of their lives; their lack of interpenetration (of facing each other) cannot sustain the needed relationship of "talk," in which the unstated mystery of the center is contained. That mystery is the original difference of man and woman, the fecund difference of marriage. Her vertigo, then, is a historical instance of the ironic *dédoublement* of language, of the reversal of the fall into time. The history of Paterson, New Jersey, those texts which haunt the Doc in the early version and provide detail like the story of Patch and Mrs. Cumming, suggests a mysterious and inviolable origin, like the whirlpool beneath the falls, that simultaneously beckons and resists. This origin is only remembered, like a trace that ambiguously signifies a lost power:

> A history that has, by its den in the
> rocks, bole and fangs, its own cane-brake
> whence, half hid, canes and stripes
> blending, it grins

The language of history speaks the silence of a primordial mystery, the enigmatic "grin" that is a sign of the unconcealed, not a symbol for it. It therefore marks the discontinuity between culture and nature, the blank of the interface which can only be recalled by "talk." A poet must come not to disclose the mystery or speak purely the language of the unconcealed, but to retrieve the trace of the origin from the debris of historical signs, the "complex" that is language and history.

PAUL MARIANI

The Eighth Day of Creation:
Rethinking Paterson

Even before he finished the last part of *Paterson* as he had originally conceived it—with its four-part structure—Williams was already thinking of moving his poem into a fifth book. The evidence for such a rethinking of the quadernity of *Paterson* exists in the manuscripts for Book 4, for there Williams, writing for himself, considered extending the field of the poem to write about the river in a new dimension: the Passaic as archetype, as the River of Heaven. That view of his river, however, was in 1950 premature, for Williams still had to follow the Passaic out into the North Atlantic, where, dying, it would lose its temporal identity in the sea of eternity, what Williams called the sea of blood. The processive mode of *Paterson* 1–4 achieved, however, Williams returned to the untouched key: the dimension of timelessness, the world of the imagination, the quiet, apocalyptic moment, what he referred to as the eighth day of creation.

The need for imaginatively apprehending such a dimension had impressed itself on Williams in several ways: two operations in 1946, a heart attack in early 1948, and the first of a series of crippling strokes which began in 1951 and continued thereafter with increasing violence until his death in 1963. The impulse for summing up the life of the man/city Paterson in the mode of the eighth day of creation—a gesture that finds its analogue in the image of a Troilus viewing his Cress and his embattled city from the seventh sphere—is no doubt anterior to these repeated intimations of immortality, but such accidents did reinforce the necessity for a new mode of saying, and, with it, a new way of seeing. But per-

From *Twentieth Century Literature* 21, no. 3 (1975). © 1975 by Hofstra University Press.

haps "new" verges on an unnecessary immensity, since it does not place the emphasis precisely where it belongs. "Life's processes are very simple," Williams wrote in his late thirties. "One or two moves are made and that is the end. The rest is repetitious." So the apocalyptic mode is not really *new* for Williams in the sense that basically new strategies were developed for the late poems. Williams had tried on the approach to the apocalyptic moment any number of times; so, for example, he destroyed the entire world, imaginatively, at the beginning of *Spring and All* to begin all over again, in order that his few readers might see the world as new. And in *Paterson* 3, the city is once again destroyed in the imagination by the successive inroads of wind, fire, and flood, necessary purgings before Dr. Paterson can discover the scarred beauty, the beautiful black Kora, in the living hell of the modern city. These repeated de-creations are necessary, in terms of Williams's psychopoetics, in order to come at that beauty locked in the imagination. "To refine, to clarify, to intensify that eternal moment in which we alone live there is but a single force," Williams had insisted in *Spring and All*. That single force was the imagination and this was its book. But *Spring and All* was only *one* of its books or, better, perhaps, *all* of Williams's books are one book, and all are celebrations of the erotic/creative power of the imagination.

What *is* new about the late poems is Williams's more relaxed way of saying and with it a more explicit way of seeing the all-pervasive radiating pattern at the core of so much that Williams wrote. In fact, all of *Paterson* and *Asphodel* and much else that Williams wrote, from *The Great American Novel* (which finds its organizing principle in the final image of the machine manufacturing shoddy products from cast-off materials, the whole crazy quilt held together with a stitched-in design) to "Old Doc Rivers" (which constructs a cubist portrait of an old-time doctor from Paterson by juggling patches of secondhand conversations, often unreliable, with old hospital records), to "The Clouds" (which tries to come at Williams's sense of loss for his father by juxtaposing images of clouds with fragmentary scenes culled from his memory), in all of these works and in others Williams presents discrete objects moving "from frame to frame without perspective / touching each other on the canvas" to "make up the picture." In this quotation Williams is describing the technique of the master of the Unicorn Tapestries, but it serves to describe perfectly his own characteristic method of presentation. It was a method he learned not only by listening attentively to Rimbaud, Stein, and Pound, but by having watched such cubist masters as Picasso and Juan Gris and Braque in the years following the Armory Show. "The truth is," Wallace Stevens remarked in an essay called "The Relations between Poetry and Painting" which he read at the Museum of Modern Art in January 1951, "The truth is that there seems to exist a corpus of remarks in respect to paintings, most often the remarks of painters themselves, which are as significant to poets as to painters . . . because they are, after all, sayings about art." Williams would have agreed wholeheartedly.

It is, specifically, this cubist mode, eschewing the fictions of perspective for a strategy of multiple centers mirroring one another, that suggests Williams's radical departure from a logocentric poetics, such as we find in the poems of Hart Crane or T. S. Eliot. So, for example, in the late winter of 1938, Williams uses Dante's *Divina Commedia* and "the fat archpriest" of Hita's *El Libro de Buen Amor* as analogues, modes for two antithetical traditions: the tradition exemplified by T. S. Eliot (Williams's archenemy) and Williams's own tradition. Dante, Williams felt, had laced himself too tightly within the constrictions of two formal "necessities": the philosophical and theological underpinnings that everywhere ground the *Comedy*, and the triadic mode of the *terza rima*. But the Spanish priest, with his looser, episodic structure and his "flat-footed quadruple rhyme scheme," placed no barriers between himself and his imagination. What Williams sensed in the priest's open form was a texture that at least manured "the entire poetic field." There was in his poem a tolerance for the imperfect, "a glowing at the center which extends in all directions equally, resembling in that the grace of Paradise." Whether that phrase describes *The Book of Love* or not, it neatly encapsulates two of Williams's long poems: *Asphodel* and *Paterson 5*. (It also describes the *Pictures from Brueghel* sequence read as parts of a single poem, but since Williams was returning in the very late work to the sharper, more nervous mode of *Spring and All*, was in a sense leaving Paradise by the back door, they belong to another meditation.)

The formal emphasis we are searching for might be phrased this way: what marks poems like *Asphodel* and *Paterson 5* as different from his earlier poetry is that Williams has come out on the other side of the apocalyptic moment. He stands, now, at a remove from the processive nature of the earlier poetry, in a world where linear time—the flow of the river—has given way to the figure of the poet standing above the river or on the shore: in either case, he is removed from the violent flux, from the frustrations of seeing the river only by fits and starts. Now the whole falls into a pattern: in Book 5 Paterson is seen by Troilus/ Williams from the Cloisters at Fort Tryon Park, the line of the river flowing quietly toward the sea, the city itself visible as a pattern of shades, a world chiming with that of the Unicorn Tapestries, the world of art that has survived. From this heavenly world, the old poet can allow himself more space for rumination, for quiet meditation. It is a world that still contains many of the jagged patterns of Williams's own world of the early fifties: the Rosenberg trial, the cold war, Mexican prostitutes and G.I.s stationed in Texas, letters from old friends and young poets. But all of these are viewed with a detached philosophical air, as parts of a pattern that are irradiated by the energy of the imagination.

For it is Kora who, revealed in the late work, glows at the center of the poetry, extending her light generously and tolerantly "in all directions equally." It is Kora again who, like the Beautiful Thing of *Paterson* 3, illuminates the poem, but it is a Kora apprehended now quite openly as icon, the source of permanent radiance: the fructifying image of the woman, the anima so many artists have celebrated in a gesture that Williams characterizes as a figure dancing satyrically, goat-footed, in measure before the female of the imagination. Now, in old age, Williams too kneels before the woman who remains herself frozen, a force as powerful and as liberating as Curie's radium, supplying light and warmth to all the surrounding details, tolerantly, democratically.

The icon presupposes a kind of paradise, or, conversely, most paradises are peopled at least at strategic points with figures approaching iconography. Dante for one felt this. It is no accident, then, that, as Williams moves into that geographical region of the imagination where the river of heaven flows, he will find other artists who have also celebrated the light. And there, in the place of the imagination expressly revealed, will be the sensuous virgin pursued by the one-horned beast, the unicorn/artist, himself become an icon in this garden of delights. Three points demand our attention, then: (1) the movement toward the garden of the imagination, where it is always spring; (2) the encounter with the beautiful thing, Kora, the sensuous virgin to whom the artist pays homage; (3) the figure of the artist, both the all-pervasive creator who contains within himself the garden and the virgin and also the willing victim, a figure moving through the tapestry, seeking his own murder and rebirth in the imagination.

First, then, the fitful but insistent movement in the late poetry toward paradise, toward what Williams called the river of heaven, the Passaic seen in its eternal phase. While Williams was at Yaddo in July and August of 1950, writing furiously to complete the last book of *Paterson* as he had until then conceived of it—as a four-part structure—Nicolas Calas (another poet and artist-in-residence at the colony and an old acquaintance of Williams) showed him the work he had been doing on Hieronymus Bosch's fifteenth-century triptych, the *Garden of Delights*. Calas had pored over every inch of Bosch's work with microscopic care, using hundreds of photographic close-ups to examine the plenitude of detail that makes up the painting. As Williams read through Calas's commentary—his working papers—which attempted to decipher the painting's total complex of meanings, Williams was "appalled," as he said in the *Autobiography*, at the sheer amount of scholarship that had been brought to bear on this medieval artifact. Calas's study of Bosch's apocalyptic icons stuck with Williams. A year later, in August 1951, while he was still recovering from the stroke he had suffered in March, Williams wrote an appreciation of Calas's achievement in giving the modern world a contemporary Bosch. "It makes the 15th century come alive to us in a way which is vivid with contemporary preoccupations," Williams wrote (Calas). It was *not* the revelation of the *medieval* imagination that Calas had stressed, but the *timeless* imagination. Here was one of the old masters whose way of seeing his fifteenth-century world differed only in accidentals from twentieth-century man's way of looking at his own world. Calas had made Bosch's mind work "as if it were a contemporary mind," and—Williams threw out in an important parenthetical aside—"we know the mind has always worked the same" (Calas). In this view, then, Bosch was brother to the surrealists, whose chief importance, Williams had said elsewhere, was that they too had managed, through the use of free association, to liberate the imagination.

And Bosch was also brother to the cubists. In presenting his subjects without worrying about the illusion of perspective, a later preoccupation inherited from the Renaissance, he, like other old masters, had refused, like Williams, to see time as predominantly linear, or, even worse, progressive. What Williams discovered was that the old masters had had their own way of transcending the idiocy of the single, fixed perspective. Like the cubists with their multiple perspectives, their discrete planes apprehended simultaneously, the old masters had also moved their subjects outside the fixed moment. They were able, therefore, to free themselves to present their figures in all of their particularity both within a specific moment and at the same time as universal types or patterns, moving frequently to the level of icon. This shift in perspective helps to explain the similarity (*and* difference) between the achievement, say, of a volume like *Spring and All* and the later poems: the analogue, except in terms of scope, is between the cubist perspectives of a still life by Juan Gris and the multiple perspectives of the unicorn tapestries centered around the central icons of the virgin and the unicorn.

But what apparently struck the most responsive chord in Williams was that Bosch, in Calas's judgment, had managed to achieve the eighth day of creation, the apocalyptic vision itself, had in fact managed to annihilate time, to be in at the end, to see the pattern of his whole life as something accomplished, the artist looking in upon his own world and finding himself there. "Men do not die if their meaning is kept alive by their work," Williams wrote in the same essay, with an eye turned on himself, "hence the masters secreted their meaning in their paintings to live" (Calas). Williams was willing to acknowledge the need for the hermetic nature of Bosch's painting, which, elucidated by the teachings of St. Augustine and St. Gregory, pointed toward "the disastrous effects of the teachings of heresy generally over against the solid foundation in virtues of the true church" (Calas). But the *particular* force of the triptych came from the face looming out of the right corner, much larger than any other and the only face in the painting showing any particular character. This nearly disembodied face was, according to Calas (and Williams agreed) the face of the artist himself, looking back "with a half suspected smile . . . directly at the beholder" (Calas). This face, peering out from the mass of hundreds of fantastic and monstrous details, amounted to a "confession" of sorts, the artist revealing his subconscious world with all of its attendant erotic fantasies. Together, the hundreds of human and animal and abstract figures, many of them frankly sexual, provided an explanation or, better, an "evocation" into the inner reality of Bosch himself. In revealing or confessing himself so fully, Bosch had transcended the limitations of the self, giving those who could read him an intimate glimpse into themselves as well. Here was a "picture of how a contemporary mind, with all its shiftings as in the subconscious, in dreams, in the throes of composition, works" (Calas).

In a sense, then, Bosch, like Williams, had read Freud's *Interpretation of Dreams* to good advantage. The left triptych represents the earthly paradise, the only kind, finally, Williams was concerned with. And there Christ, the figure of the Creator, is about to present the virgin, Kora, as Eve, to the bridegroom. In that primal gesture, Bosch seems to suggest, nature has begun to manifest its tensions. Already death has entered the garden; the monstrous, as in the two-legged dog, has infiltrated Bosch's world. Williams's garden of delights in *Asphodel* contains the same kinds of potential tensions, but all are presented tolerantly, all, even the damned, sharing the light of the imagination. Bosch's triptych, I suggest, then, chimes with Williams's *Asphodel*, a poem in three parts and a coda. Both are, basically, confessions; both present a series of discrete images held on the same plane by the artist. Linearity is eschewed for a mode of cubist simultaneity, and both poem and painting contain versions of the garden. Moreover, if one "reads" Bosch not from left to right but as one might read one's image in a mirror, in reverse, then one begins with the artist in hell and moves to a new beginning, with the bridegroom beholding the luminous bride, the sensuous virgin, apprehended on the eighth day as in the primal garden.

In originally conceiving of *Paterson* in four parts, Williams had, as he pointed out, added Pan to the embrace of the Trinity, much as he felt Dante had unwittingly done in supplying a "fourth unrhymed factor, unobserved" to the very structure of the *Commedia*. (This factor appears if we note the creative dissonance developed by the unrhymed ending reappearing in any four lines after the initial four.) The world of *Paterson* 1–4 is very much a world in flux, a world in violent, haphazard process, where objects washing in or crashing against the surfaces of the man/city Paterson are caught up into the pattern of the poem even as they create in turn the pattern itself. So such things as the chance appearance of a nurse who was discovered to have a case of *Salmonella montevideo*, written up into a case history in the *Journal of the American Medical Association* for July 29, 1948, or a letter from a young unknown poet from Paterson named Allen Ginsberg, or a hasty note scribbled by Ezra Pound from St. Elizabeth's

Hospital in Washington, letters from Marcia Nardi or Fred Miller or Josephine Herbst or Edward Dahlberg or Alva Turner find their way into the action painting of the poem. The lines too are jagged, hesitant, coiling back on themselves, for the most part purposely flat, only in "isolate flecks" rising to the level of a lyricism that seems without artificiality or undue self-consciousness, a language shaped from the mouths of Polish mothers, but heightened.

The first four books of *Paterson* are, really, in a sense, the creation of the first six days, a world caught up very much in the rapid confusion of its own linear, processive time, where the orphic poet like the carnival figure of Sam Patch must keep his difficult balance or be pulled under by the roar of the language at the brink of the descent into chaos every artist encounters in the genesis of creation. What Williams was looking for instead in a fifth book, after resting from his unfolding creation, was to see the river at the heart of his poem as the ourobouros, the serpent with its tail in its mouth, the eternal river, the river of heaven. This meant, of course, that time itself would have to change, and a new time meant a relatively new way of measuring, meant a more secure, a more relaxed way of saying. That was a question, primarily, of form, and the emphasis on the variable foot, which the critics went after all through the fifties and sixties like hounds after an elusive hare, was in large part a strategy of Williams's own devising. But it was an absolutely necessary strategy for him, because just here the real revolution in poetry would have to occur: here with the river, metaphor for the poetic line itself.

The river of heaven became almost an obsession for Williams in the early fifties. First he had considered viewing *Paterson* 4 under that rubric; then he had begun a long poem called *The River of Heaven*, which became instead *Asphodel*. In June 1950, Allen Ginsberg had written Williams (in a letter that finds itself caught in the grid of *Paterson* 4) that he'd been "walking the streets of Paterson and discovering the bars." "I wonder," he asked, "if you have seen River Street most of all, because that is really at the heart of what is to be known." There were a number of bars along River Street, especially in the black section, which he recommended to Williams in the summer of 1952. "What I want of your son," Williams wrote Louis Ginsberg, "is for him to take me to a bar on River Street. . . . I don't know what the joint is like or whether we'd be welcome there but if it's something to experience and to see I'd like to see it for I want to make it the central locale for a poem which I have in mind—a sort of extension of *Paterson*." From River Street, one of the oldest streets in Paterson, which follows the course of the Passaic, Williams could view through the painted glass of an old tavern-turned-bar the Passaic River surrounded by a cosmic harmony of sorts: the dance of the satyrs, swinging to jazz, on the eighth day of creation. Things have a way of changing, however, and the river of heaven finds its enactment not in the back room of the Bobaloo, but as it flows through the unicorn tapestries, the unicorn emerging from its waters, having escaped the silent hounds, threaded teeth bared, baying his imminent murder.

"Maybe there'll be a 5th book of Paterson embodying everything I've learned of 'the line' to date," Williams told Robert Lowell in March 1952. And, indeed, much of the new book does incorporate Williams's late development with the line, including the three-ply line of *Asphodel*. But the manuscripts reveal an interesting change in Williams's collage for Book 5, which refocuses the emphasis of the entire book and brings us from the river to the icon. Williams had intended to include a long letter to him from Cid Corman dealing with the whole question of modern prosody and, in fact, even in the galleys, he had included that letter. But in its place Williams inserted at the last minute a letter from Edward Dahlberg that he had received in late September 1957 when he was putting the finishing touches on Book 5.

What Williams saw in Dahlberg's letter was a modern, living, breathing analogue for Brueghel's *The Adoration of the Kings* in the Danish woman surrounded by the police, and the placement of Dahlberg's letter focuses the attention away from the question of the line (which had in any event been attended to by Sappho and Bessie Smith) and onto the modern representation of the central icon of Book 5, the beautiful thing, Kora. It is the icon that includes, really, all of her sisters, from the "young woman / with rounded brow" who listens to the "hunter's horn" and who alone can lure the unicorn-poet, to Williams's own English grandmother (whose presence had marked his initiation into the filthy Passaic forty years before and who rounds off the conclusion of *Paterson*). And it includes as well the virgin in Lorca's *The Love of Don Perlimplín*, Osamu Dazai's saintly sister, "tagged" by her lover in *The Setting Sun*, those Mexican whores turning up their dresses in a short sketch by a young writer named Gilbert Sorrentino who had sent Williams his manuscript for the poet's comments, a young girl Williams remembered who'd gone swimming naked with him and all the boys at Sandy Bottom some sixty years before, and, finally, Sappho singing and Bessie Smith singing and the 3,000 years between them now as nothing.

In his 1928 novel, *A Voyage to Pagany*, Williams removed what is in fact the central chapter because the editors found the book too long to print in its original form. That chapter, "The Venus," describes a scene between a young fräulein and Dev (for Evans Dionysius) Evans. There the American doctor and the German girl sit in a quiet spot south of Rome which still bears evidences of having been in some remote past a pagan grotto, while Evans tries to explain the elusive beauty he is searching for in America. It is clear from Williams's description that Evans is in fact speaking to a modern-day incarnation of Venus herself, specifically Botticelli's sensuous virgin. But this Venus is about to enter a convent because she has not found the figure of the artist who can fully liberate her, although Evans's new-world paganism attracts her. The steady glance of this German Venus continued to haunt Williams, and he found that glance again in the figure of another Venus in a garb very like a nun's: Brueghel's Virgin. A buxom German peasant girl, she holds her baby boy upon her knee, as later, in the *Pictures from Brueghel*, she will pose in icon fashion, detached from the quotidian bustle everywhere apparent, as she does too in Giotto's *Adoration of the Magi*, which Williams celebrated in "The Gift," a poem also from the mid-fifties.

It is she, Kora, around whom all of *Paterson 5* radiates, and, in the tapestries, she appears again with the tamed unicorn amidst a world of flowers where Williams had always felt at home. In a sense, Marianne Moore's real toad in an imaginary garden finds its correlative here in Williams's icons of the virgin/whore situated among "the sweetsmelling primrose / growing close to the ground," "the slippered flowers / crimson and white, / balanced to hang on slender bracts," forget-me-nots, dandelions, love-in-a-mist, daffodils, and gentians, and daisies. We have seen this woman before: she is the woman in *Asphodel* caring for her flowers in winter, in hell's despite, another German Venus, Floss Williams. Which, then, is the real, Williams's wife seen or his icon of the wife? And his wife seen now, at this moment, or his wife remembered, an icon released by the imagination from time, ageless, this woman containing all women? Rather, it is the anima, the idea of woman, with its tenuous balance between the woman glimpsed and the woman realized, the hag language whored and whored again but transformed by the poet-lover's desire into something virginal and new, the woman and the language translated to the eighth day of creation, assuming a new condition of dynamic permanence. In this garden, the broken, jagged, random things of Williams's world are caught up in a pattern, a dance where the poem, like the tapestries themselves, can be possessed a thousand thousand times and yet remain as fresh and as virginal as on the day they were conceived, like Venus, from the head of their creator.

The woman is of course all-pervasive in Williams's poems. What is different now is the more explicit use of Kora as the symbol, in fact, the central icon in the late poems. Two examples from the earlier sections of *Paterson* will serve to illustrate differences in the handling of his women. In *Paterson* 1, Williams sketches the delineaments of the giants, the female of the place, Garrett Mountain, resting against the male of it, the city of Paterson. "Paterson," the genesis of Book 1 begins, "lies in the valley under the Passaic Falls / its spent waters forming the outline of his back," Over "against him, stretches the low mountain / The Park's her head, carved, above the Falls, by the quiet river. . . ." Williams, as Michael Weaver has noted, may even have had Pavel Tchelitchew's *Fata Morgana*, his painting of two reclining earth figures, a man, a woman, in mind. This pattern of the unroused lovers is evoked obliquely later in Book 2 when Paterson/

Williams, walking on Garrett Mountain, notices a young couple lying partly concealed by some bushes, intent on each other while Sunday strollers float past them on all sides:

> But the white girl, her head
> upon an arm, a butt between her fingers
> lies under the bush
>
> Semi-naked, facing her, a sunshade
> over his eyes,
> he talks with her
>
> the jalopy half hid
> behind them in the trees —
> I bought a new bathing suit, just
>
> pants and a brassier:
> the breasts and
> the pudenda covered — beneath
>
> the sun in frank vulgarity.
> Minds beaten thin
> by waste — among
>
> the working classes SOME sort
> of breakdown
> has occurred.

Mural has become cameo, but the image of reclining lovers remains, substantially unchanged. In terms of strategy, however, Williams has purposely not pressed his parallel home. For the attention must be riveted first on the actuality of the encounter: it is midmorning in late May, probably 1942 or '43. Or for that matter '33 or '73. These are probably young second-generation Polish- or Italian-Americans, surprised by eros on this, their day off, intent on seizing the day before returning to the silk mills or locomotive works in the industrial town sprawled out below them. But for this moment, the pattern of young lovers persists as archetype, fleshed out in these particular working-class people who impinge upon Williams's consciousness.

There is another interesting image that Williams found *too* explicit to finally place in Book 4, but the various manuscripts for that book mention it several times. In the modern Idyll that begins *Paterson* 4, Williams gives us a strange love triangle that spells frustration from whatever angle of incidence we follow: the love triangle between Corydon, an aging, lame lesbian and would-be poetess, well educated in the classics and in French literature, whose penthouse apartment in the East 50s overlooks the river; her masseuse, a young (twenty-one-year-old) nurse from Ramapo (perhaps a Jackson White) trained at Passaic General Hospital in Paterson (where Williams served for some forty years), and Dr. Paterson himself, that married man and aging lover. Paterson is driven wild by the young virgin's beauty; indeed he cannot even think unless she first removes her clothes. For Williams she is, explicitly, the very incarnation of Goya's famous Maja Desnuda. And if for Dr. Paterson she remains the elusive new-world beauty who cannot give herself to the new-world poet but follows instead the old-world hag (Europe) into a world cold and alien, she is first and foremost a real woman, someone from Williams's own past, an incarnation of the unattainable reclining nude, the odalisque, Olympia, more fleshly cousin of Stevens's Mrs. Pappadoppoulos. Goya's nude seems to have informed Williams's realization of Phyllis in the unpublished sheets of the Idyll, but Williams carefully removed the scaffolding in the published version.

Paterson 5 eschews such oblique stratagems, however. Williams has made that consummate metapoem far more explicit for several reasons, one comes to realize: first, because no critic, not even the most friendly and the most astute, had even begun to adequately sound the real complexities of the poem by 1956, ten years after *Paterson* 1 appeared. (Indeed an adequate critical vocabulary for the kind of thing Williams was doing does not seem to have been available then to the critics and reviewers.) Second, Williams felt the need to praise his own tradition, his own pantheon of artists, to pay tribute to those others who had also helped to celebrate the light. Williams would show that, on the eighth day of creation, all of the disparate, jagged edges of *Paterson* could, as he had said in his introduction, multiply themselves and so reduce themselves to unity, to a dance around the core of the imagination.

In the dreamlike worlds of *Asphodel* and *Paterson* 5, filled as they are with the radiant light of the imagination, all disparate images revolve around the virgin/whore, including the "male of it," the phallic artist who is both earthly Pan and unicorn, that divine lover, who dances contrapuntally against his beloved. Williams, perhaps sensing that the old, crude fight against the clerks of the great tradition had been sufficiently won by that point to let him relax, chooses now to celebrate a whole pantheon of old masters in *Asphodel* and again in *Paterson* 5.

And if the presences of Bosch, Brueghel, and the master of the unicorn tapestries are the central presences in the three late long poems, still, there is room to celebrate a host of other artists who dance in attendance on the woman as well. We can do little more at this point than enumerate some of them: Toulouse-Lautrec, who painted the very human turn-of-the-century Parisian prostitutes among whom he lived; Gauguin, celebrating his sorrowful reclining nude in *The Loss of Virginity*; the anonymous Inca sculptor who created the statuette of a woman at her bath some 3,000 years ago; the 6,000-year-old cave paintings of bison; Cézanne for his patches of blue and blue; Daumier, Picasso, Juan Gris, Gertrude Stein, Kung; Albrecht Dürer for his *Melancholy*; Audubon, Ben Shahn, and Marsden Hartley.

We come, then, finally, to our third point: the figure of the artist himself, the male principle incessantly attracted to and moving toward the female of it: the anima. And here we are confronted with the comic and the grotesque: the figure of Sam Patch or the hydrocephalic dwarf or the Mexican peasant in Eisenstein's film, and, in the late poems, the portrait of the old man, all of these finding their resolution and comic apotheosis in the captive, one-horned unicorn, a figure, like the figure of the satyr erectus, of the artist's phallic imagination. There is, too, Brueghel's self-portrait, as Williams thought, re-created in the first of Williams's own pictures taken from Brueghel, and imitated in a cubist mode. That old man, with his "Bulbous nose" (one thinks of Williams's own early poem celebrating his own nose) and his "eyes red-rimmed / from over-use" with "no time for any / thing but his painting." And, again, there is the head of the old smiling Dane, the Tollund man, seen in a photograph; it is a portrait of a man, a sacrificial victim, strangled as part of some forgotten spring rite, the features marvelously preserved intact by the tanning effects of the bogs from which he had been exhumed after twenty centuries of strong silence, that 2,000-year-old face frozen into something like a half-smile. That face chimes with Brueghel's face as both chime with the strange, half-smiling face of Bosch peering out from his strange world where order has given way to an apocalyptic nightmare.

But the male remains the lesser figure of the two in Williams. As he told Theodore Roethke in early 1950, "All my life I have hated my face and wanted to smash it." (It was one reason, he told Roethke in the same letter, that he could not even bear to speak of Vivienne Koch's critical study of him which had just appeared. What mattered was not the man himself, but the man's work.) He was willing, however, to let the icon of the unicorn, the one-horned beast, stand. And he let it stand because it represented the necessary male complement to the female of it, the object desired, the beautiful thing: the language in its impossible edenic state. No one but the virgin can tame the unicorn, the legend goes, and Williams had, like other artists before and after him, given himself up to that elusive beauty. Like Hart Crane in another mode, he had given himself up to be murdered, to offer himself not, as Pound had, to the pale presences of the past, virtually all of them male voices, but for the virgin, Kora. And yet, there was a way out, a hole at the bottom of the pit for the artist, in the timeless world of the imagination, the enchanted circle, the jeweled collar encircling the unicorn's neck. In the final tapestry of the series, the unicorn kneels within the fence paling, (pomegranates bespeak fertility and the presence of Kora), at ease among a panoply of flowers forever on the eighth day of creation, a world evoked for Williams out of the imagination, the source from which even the author of Revelation must have created his own eighth day in his time.

What was of central importance to Williams was not the artist, then, whose force is primarily directional and whose presence is in any event everywhere, but the icon that motivates the artist and urges him on: the icon of Kora, the image of the beloved. And this figure appears, of course, everywhere in Williams's writing, assuming many faces, yet always, finally one. Asked in his mid-seventies what it was that kept him writing, Williams answered that it was all for the young woman whose eyes he had caught watching him out there in some audience as he read his poems. It was all for lovely Sappho, then, and all for Venus. Consider for a moment the example of other modern poets: Yeats's Helen of Troy, Stevens's fat, voluptuous mundo, or Pound, finding a shadow of his ideal beauty in the *yeux glauques*, the lacquered eyes of Jenny in those Burne-Jones cartoons, or the eyes of the goddess momentarily penetrating through the very walls of Pound's tent at the U. S. Army Detention Center at Pisa in that summer of '45. With them Williams places his own icon of the woman rising out of the hell of his own repressions. In the world of art, in that garden where spring is a condition of permanence, where the earthly garden chimes perfectly with the garden of paradise, the eye of the unicorn is still and still intent upon the woman.

DONALD HALL

William Carlos Williams
and the Visual

Nantucket

Flowers through the window
lavender and yellow

changed by white curtains—
Smell of cleanliness—

Sunshine of late afternoon—
On the glass tray

a glass pitcher, the tumbler
turned down, by which

a key is lying—And the
immaculate white bed

When I began reading poetry, early in the 1940s, William Carlos Williams was old news. At a bookstore, I picked up a copy of *New Directions 1937*: with Henry Miller, John Wheelwright, Gertrude Stein, E. E. Cummings, William Saroyan, Richard Eberhart, Delmore Schwartz, Kenneth Rexroth—and Williams's "Paterson: Episode 17," the marvelous "Beautiful Thing" poem. But by the end of the decade I was studying at college under new critics, reading Blackmur and Empson, doing *explication de text* with enthusiasm. We practiced on the well-surveyed countries of John Donne and T. S. Eliot; we talked Eliot all day and wrote Eliot all night. Whitman was off-bounds, impossible, an embarrassment, the crazy cousin at the dinner party.

From *Field* 29 (Fall 1983). © 1983 by Oberlin College.

But what did we do with William Carlos Williams?

When I say "we," of course, I exclude Robert Creeley, Charles Olson, Cid Corman, Louis Zukofsky, and others who knew what to do with him—who attended not only to his poems but to his theory. "We" is the rest, who swam with the new critical tide and found it exhilarating. Like Thomas Hardy, Williams wrote poems which made it hard for us to explicate intellectual complexity. We knew poems about a red wheelbarrow, the road to the contagious hospital, and yachts, from anthologies like Untermeyer's and Williams's. A teacher loaned me a copy of *The Wedge*. I bought *The Pink Church*. I *liked* him; everybody claimed to like him—but I don't think we read him very well.

It was the convention then to praise Williams for his *eye*. Out of recollections of Imagism, or what Imagism might have been, we praised him and pigeonholed him. We condescended by admiring him—and we ignored his inventions. Book One of *Paterson* made some of us take notice: later books of *Paterson* rewarded attention less. When he wrote the late, triadic poems, many readers responded with more enthusiasm. It is still the late poetry—the excellent Wisdom Literature which Williams turned to in his age—by which he is best known, and not by the characteristic early work. For me, his early work remains the most shocking and the most useful. "Nantucket" is typical of the early work— short, stark, clear, relentless, ecstatic, with purity of speech and great delicacy of sound.

Put "Nantucket" up against "A Valediction: Forbidding Mourning" or "Lycidas" or "Ode to a Nightingale" or "Dover Beach." Or put it against "The Love Song of J. Alfred Prufrock," for that matter, with its honeyed Tennysonian conclusion; put it against "Sunday Morning." If we measure a centipede against a Japanese beetle, both are tolerably insects. But how are "Nantucket" and "Epithalamion" both *poems*? These other poems assemble lines and images into an order of thinking, appropriately complex, pendulum-arcs along the true path of ambivalence. But "Nantucket" does not perform on this path. If you come to it out of literary history (as opposed to reading with the naked eye, which is always in short supply) it looks like something you might call Imagism, and you start talking about "eye."

In reality, "Nantucket" has little to do with the movement which Hulme and Flint cooked up in London before the Great War; nor does it resemble H. D.'s early lyrics, nor Pound's from the time of *Des Imagistes*. In early Williams, maybe because of his rejection of his English father, his emphasis falls not on visual description but on the gestures of American speech, on the poem's visual shape which enforces rhythm, and on something which we might call a painterly stasis.

"Nantucket" has eye enough. But the visual adjectives are general: "yellow," "white," "white" again; also the nouns: "curtains," "sunshine," "tumbler," "a key . . ." Williams does not write about an oblong-ended, brass, Yale key; the curtains are white but they are neither lace nor linen nor printed nor wrinkled nor ironed. When he writes of "yellow / changed by . . .", the past participle is indirectly visual; the word asks recollection to color the curtain, and the reader to alter the tints of flowers as white curtains alter them. He does the same, in another area of sense, with "Smell of cleanliness," giving us no sense-image or metaphor, speaking in general or abstract language. Williams is master of abstract language; "no ideas but in things" has no things in it, only ideas.

It is by his absences that we know a poet. Williams's absence of striking particularities, and of unusual word-combinations and metaphors, make a gesture of simplicity and naturalness in diction, speech-likeness. This is the true shock of Williams; he writes plain talk. He writes nouns and adjectives, no verbs except "is lying" and the past participles of "changed" and "turned"; not much action here: the vision is breathless with nouns. Egalitarian diction—no word better than its neighbor!—sets up "immaculate" to crash like a thunderball. Of course this violates egalitarianism. Why use egalitarianism unless you violate it?

Although a tradition of English and American poets—like Crabbe, Wordsworth, and Frost, Whitman to a degree—uses the demotic, Williams in the twenties and thirties was the most shocking. And he used it in connection with his other absence—of ideas. Now idea-less-ness is not unprecedented, but critics and professors teach and write about ideas rather than poems, which leaves idealess poems off the agenda. Of course ideas are perfectly fine objects to stuff into the container of the poem: one may add old shoes, emotions, industrial waste . . . Poems contain everything like (in the words of the poet) the stomach of the shark. Mother Goose is a wonderful poet not notable for ideas. The academic neglect of Thomas Hardy's great poems derives from the difficulty teachers find in discussing poems that lack difficulty. Even Keats, in "To Autumn," writes a poem almost immaculate of idea. Of course Keats's ode is not without suggestions of value; it makes statement by shape—a quality we find in music, in Greek vases, in architectural design, in painting and sculpture, and for that matter in poems of intellectual content.

"To Autumn," of course, does not share "Nantucket's" other absence—of unusual or unusually arranged language; for a poem that shares both absences we need another American. Look at Whitman, not always, but here:

A Farm Picture

Through the ample open door of the peaceful country barn,
A sunlit pasture field with cattle and horses feeding,
And haze and vista, and the far horizon fading away.

What a lovely small poem. One must qualify with a word like "small" and one must be sure that the qualification is not condescension . . . Or let me condescend to "A Farm Picture" and to "Nantucket" only by acknowledging that they are not so ambitious as "Out of the Cradle Endlessly Rocking" nor "Paterson Book One." We may love Herrick without calling "Upon Julia's Clothes" as great a poem as "The Garden." And in poems like "Nantucket," "Upon Julia's Clothes," and "Bah-bah Black Sheep" we begin to isolate poetry; it is more difficult to isolate the *poetry* of "Church Monuments" because ideas and theology distract us.

Williams makes me think of Herrick in other ways. Both give us models of joyous world-love. In "Nantucket" and in many other poems, Williams enacts a joy—unpretentious, accomplished in action not in reflection—like Herrick's double pleasure in Julia's motions and in the language by which he embodies her motions. Now Williams takes delight in his words also; no one is so scrupulous in movement of line-break and rhyme: "yell*ow*" picks up "wind*ow*" and harks back to "flow*ers*"; consonants from "curtains" return in "cleanliness"; the bang-bang percussive "glass tray" is followed with "glass pitch-," "turned down," and "white bed" . . .

In "Nantucket" *ear* does ten times what *eye* does. If we try a portion in paragraph form—saying it aloud as if we were reading from the newspaper—we have: "On the glass tray a glass pitcher, the tumbler turned down, by which a key is lying . . ." Nothing. The line on the page does the thing, providing we hear it according to its visual shape, the lines controlling rhythm and enforcing speech-likeness. In the next to last line, he places a neat pause between "the . . ." and the thunderball "immaculate"—then swiftly bang-bangs his coda: "white bed." Sound is scored by Williams's re-invention of the page.

The re-invention of the page. In *this* sense—a visual method for capturing speech—maybe Williams's eye was as important as we said, forty years ago. Let me try setting Whitman's "A Farm Picture" into lines that imitate Williams's spacing. (My version is arbitrary; other breaks might do just as well or better.) I omit capitals, respell "thru," omit two copulas, and come up with:

> thru the ample
> open door of
>
> the peaceful country
> barn, a sunlit
>
> pasture field
> with cattle and

> horses feeding,
> haze, vista, and the
>
> far horizon
> fading away

If it does not seem to resemble Williams, I mistake my point—which is double: first, the absences of Whitman's poem anticipate Williams (so does its emphatic stasis, which I will mention in a moment); second, the characteristic visual arrangement of Williams's early work—with all its pausing—provides a considerable part of the stylistic signature. Of course this Whitman poem, mistreated, lacks Williams's characteristic intimacies of sound, especially his frequent rhyming.

We need say one more thing about "Nantucket." Like many poems by Williams, it takes pleasure in stasis. Meister Eckhart among other mystics tells us what the soul longs for: repose. It is worth noticing the relationship to still-life, and recollecting Williams's closeness to his painter-friends. It is also worth remarking that for many poets painting is the second art. The perspective of painting-values, as it were misapplied to the time-art of poetry, suggests or necessitates a useful conflict, as words-in-motion command stillness.

"A Farm Picture" and "Nantucket" provide repose. I compared "Nantucket" to "To Autumn" for its absence of ideas; Williams's poem also resembles Keats's in the value it suggests for the experience it embodies. This Williams poem does not begin by saying "so much depends / upon" but such insistence is implicit: an intense, even ecstatic value placed upon the act of total attention, stasis become ecstasis, and soul flies out of body in astonished, acute notation of experience.

JOHN W. ERWIN

William Carlos Williams
and Europe

*He claims American birth, but I strongly suspect that he emerged on
shipboard just off Bedloe's Island and that his dark and serious eyes gazed
up in their first sober contemplation at the Statue and its brazen and
monstrous nightshirt. . . . One might accuse him of being, blessedly, the
observant foreigner, perceiving American vegetation and landscape quite
directly, as something put there for him to look at.*

—EZRA POUND

*P*aterson amply justifies Pound's claim that William Carlos Williams was always
the intruding tourist. As a poet, Williams was no more exclusively American
than Eliot or Pound were European. He only learned to dramatize a distinctively
American concern for dialogue between writers and readers by achieving something like the mastery of foreign languages which he attributed to Poe.

> If there ever had been another American to use his Greek, Sanscrit,
> Hebrew, Latin, French, German, Italian and Spanish—in the text
> —with anything like the unspoiled mastery of Poe, we should have
> known, long since, what it meant to have a literature of our own.

Certainly Williams announced *Paterson* as a "reply to Greek and Latin with the
bare hands" and mocked the disregard for communication in poetry written with
an eye to European tradition.

> And so about a generation ago, when under the influence of Whitman
> the prevalent verse forms had gone to the free-verse pole, the coun-
> tering cry of Order! Order! rewakened. That was the time of the new
> Anglo-Catholicism . . . Nothing can be simply beautiful, it must be

From *Lyric Apocalypse: Reconstruction in Ancient and Modern Poetry.* © 1984 by
Scholars Press.

so beautiful that no one can understand it *except* by the assistance of the cult. It must be a "mystery."

But this passage from the 1929 essay "Against the Weather: A Study of the Art" follows a criticism of Whitman in which Williams corroborated Mallarmé's critique of free verse.

Verse is measure, there is no free verse. . . . Whitman was never able to fully realize the significance of his structural innovations. As a result he fell back to the overstuffed catalogues of his later poems and a sort of looseness that was not freedom but lack of measure. Selection, structural selection was lacking.

Even though Williams sometimes became strident in his Americanism and claimed that the French were superficial readers of Poe, he followed Mallarmé in choosing Poe as a model for rigorous self-criticism in poetry. And, as we shall see, he ended *Paterson* by speaking French as well as Eliot did when he punctuated *Four Quartets* with echoes of Mallarmé more accurate and productive than Pound's variants of "pli selon pli."

Paterson bears comparison with Stevens's and Eliot's long poems. While it sometimes justifies Poe's doubts about the long poem, many of its dramatizations of interchange between poet and reader are strong enough to set beside the best sequences in *Four Quartets* and "An Ordinary Evening in New Haven." For they bring the dialectic structure of Pindar's odes up to date and reply to Greek and Latin with hands that are far from bare.

I

Early in Book I of *Paterson* Williams addressed himself: "say it! / No ideas but in things." Most readers of *Paterson* stress the message "no ideas but in things": a denial of the idealist distinction between mind and matter which has characterized Western thought since Plato and Aristotle. But the *form* of Williams's subversion—"say it!"—is just as interesting. When the poet emphatically commanded himself to deny that there is any binary conflict to mediate, he called attention to his linguistic medium and acknowledged that this abrupt negation is a moment in a dialogue with readers. In *Paterson* "ideas" are generated from complex stagings of the potential encounter between the common reader and disparate texts ("things").

Louis Martz, an outstanding exegete of the poetry of meditation, locates *Paterson* in Williams's mind:

Book V suggests that we might read *Paterson* as a kind of tapestry, woven out of memories and observations, composed by one man's imagination but written in part by his friends, whose letters are scattered throughout, by his patients, whose words are remembered throughout, and by all the milling populace of Paterson, past and present, including that unicorn in the center of the field: the Kingself, within whose mind these thoughts assemble like "a flight of birds all together, seeking their nests in the season."

But Williams's tapestry is woven more than in part by "patients." It continually requires that readers help reassemble the bird-thoughts of a fallen king—who is himself only insofar as he is a synecdochic personification of a large community. By presenting many aspirants to the role of mediatory Word who are still more obviously inadequate than Whitman's mockingbird, *Paterson* provokes us to counter a general lack of communication ("the language is missing them / they die also / incommunicado . . .").

Williams's alter ego is not articulate. Words fail N. F. Paterson ("Sam Patch") when he expects to rise like Milton's Lycidas but without the "dear might of him who walked the waves":

On the day the crowds were gathered on all sides. He appeared and made a short speech as he was wont to do. A speech! What could he say that he must leap so desperately to complete it? And plunged toward the stream below. But instead of descending with a plummet-like fall his body wavered in the air—speech had failed him. He was confused. The word had been drained of its meaning. There's no mistake in Sam Patch. He struck the water on his side and disappeared. A great silence followed as the crowd stood spellbound.

The long poem can eventually project resurrection, however, because it provides for a secular equivalent of the intense recreative dialogue between the Word and his witnesses in Scripture. As Williams had the grotesque Sam Patch double his role of show-off, he had an equally bizarre minister's wife impersonate the reader.

Having ascended the flight of stairs (the Hundred Steps) Mr. and Mrs. Cummings walked over the solid ledge to the vicinity of the cataract, charmed with the wonderful prospect . . . where thousands have stood before, and where there is a fine view of the sublime curiosities of the place. When they had enjoyed the luxury of the scene for a considerable length of time, Mr. Cummings said, "My dear, I believe it is time for us to set our face homeward"; and at the same moment, turned round in order to lead the way. He instantly heard the voice of distress, looked back and his wife was gone!

The text later implies a marriage-in-death between these self-destructive figures who represent the extremes of extroversion and introversion bred by a society which derives identity from exclusive ownership.

> Patch leaped but Mrs. Cummings shrieked
> and fell—unseen— ...
> :a body found next spring
> frozen in an ice-cake; or a body
> fished next day from the muddy swirl—

We may see this tentative association of male and female bodies respectively yielded and held by the river as a prefiguration of our exchange with Williams. As readers we join him in voluntarily giving ourselves up alternately to the endless flow of the idiom and to our common urge to freeze time into crystalline significance. When the performer's and the spectator's bodies are both joined and separated, the mix of alienation and intimacy in the relationship between writers and readers is as emphatically defined the focus of interest as it is in St. John's account of the Lamb's self-sacrificial union with the crystalline Bride Jerusalem.

Williams authorized his projections of a *Liebstod* between weird figures of himself and his readers by acknowledging that his experiment in secular apocalypse was inspired by a series of non-Scriptural variations upon the tense relationships between performers and audiences in Revelation. The speaker calls for inspiration that will save him from writing dead letters: "stale as a whale's breath: Breath! Breath!" But as an interpolated prose-fragment notes, "the artist is an Ishmael." It is in fact a whale's breath which saves *Paterson* from being stale: the long poem is structured by variations upon the domestication of Shakespearean tragedy in *Moby-Dick*. If we recognize that Williams took turns playing the indiscriminately responsive Ishmael and the compulsive show-off Ahab, we are more likely to help him rearticulate literary history and moderate Mrs. Cummings's obsession with fluid multiplicity.

Unlike the author of *Moby-Dick*, however, Williams could not expect his readers to recognize many Biblical allusions. In order to project an equivalent intensity of relationship between authority and interpreters, he had to represent both its violent and its erotic aspects more explicitly than Melville did. The dialogue of an anonymous couple provides a concentrated model for garrulous *Paterson*:

> we sit and talk
> I wish to be with you abed, we two
> as if the bed were the bed of a stream

> —I have much to say to you
> We sit and talk

Yet a poet can only compensate for the lack of generative dialogue in modern culture if he repeatedly acknowledges that poetic communication is a *coitus interruptus*. In making love with the Park upon the rock, "female to the city / —upon whose body Paterson instructs his thoughts," Paterson imitates the brash, lordly Whitman of "Song of Myself." But he is often interrupted by a female disciple who complains that he has not adequately transmitted his poetic genius to her: "the outcome of my failure with you has been the complete damming up of all my creative capacities." Similarly, an anonymous follower of undetermined sex, the reader, is to reanimate the tradition of erotic poetry by witnessing an apocalyptic destruction of a library which paradoxically assures its continuity:

> (breathing the books in)
> the acrid fumes
> for what they could decipher
> warping the sense to detect the norm, to break
> through the skull of custom

As in the Scriptural apocalypse which burns up the old world and its texts, "ideas" occur in the *destruction* of "things": in interchange between interpreters who challenge as much as they desire each other. But several more provocative replays of the grotesque mystic marriage of Patch and Mrs. Cummings more urgently invite us to help reconstruct a cohesive community of times and persons.

In an idyll set on a distinctly Lesbian shore, a female Corydon (the Virgilian counterpart of Thyrsis, model for Milton's uncouth swain in "Lycidas") tries in vain to make an eternal POEM with Phyllis—who also sports in the shade with Paterson.

> Here it is. This is what I've been leading up to It's called, *Corydon*,
> *A Pastoral.* We'll skip the first part, about the rocks and sheep, begin
> with the helicopter. You remember that?:
> . . . drives the gulls up in a cloud
> Um . . . no more woods and fields. Therefore
> present, forever present

The artificial controlled present of a colloquial pastoral only exposes the absurd recurrence of death, incarnated in a corpse also of indeterminate sex: "some student come / waterlogged to the surface following / last night's thunderstorm." However, a letter from a homosexual male poet, Allen Ginsberg, ratifies the

mock-marriage between "Corydon" and "Phyllis" and suggests that literary genesis does not follow the rhythms of nature but those of dialogue. As the new
Lycidas's sex is uncertain, Paterson's counterpart writes exclusively neither as a
son nor as a father—

> in the style of those courteous sages of yore who recognized one
> another across the generations as brotherly children of the muses. In
> Pierre and the Confidence Man my literary liking is Melville and in
> my own generation, one Jack Kerouac whose first book came out
> this year.

Quoting Ginsberg's deference to one of his own primary authorities and then
his praise for a fraternal *miglior fabbro*, Williams defined reversible exchange
between poet-readers as the primary matrix of his utterance.

This definition is further established when another female image of the
reader replaces Mrs. Cummings: a "compact black bitch" greets the godly father-
son as the resurrected image of both Sam Patch and the Lycidas-like drowned
student. Williams domesticated the ancient impulse to represent exchange between authors and interpreters even more systematically than Melville, a literary
authority he shared with Ginsberg.

> She looks to sea, cocking her ears and,
> restless, walks to the water's edge where
> she sits down, half in the water
>   Climbing the
> bank, after a few tries, he picked
> some beach plums from a low bush and
> sampled one of them, spitting the seed out,
> then headed inland, followed by the dog

Through interplay between a performer and an attentive witness, a prophetic
dissemination ("spitting the seed out") challenges the alienations of individual
persons and moments prescribed by modern secular variants of Scriptural patri-
archy. Unlikely Nausicaa to an Odysseus whom Williams was trying to save from
the bookshelves to which Pound's imitations of Andreas Divus condemned him,
the humble dog helps bring home to the American shore the concern for reciprocal exchange which animates the European literary tradition from Homer and
Pindar to Mallarmé and Celan.

Although Williams advertised the reunion of swimmer and dog as "the eternal close of the spiral / . . . the end," he later added two more turns of the screw.
Offering his text to two female interpreters, he more authoritatively located himself in the European tradition—and vice-versa. If Eliot's Tiresias throbs between

the two lives of man and woman, in *Paterson* a man/woman lives on still another Lesbian shore.

> There is a woman in our town
> walks rapidly, flat bellied
> in work slacks upon the street
> where I saw her
> > neither short
> nor tall, nor old nor young
> her
> > face would attract no
> > adolescent.
>
> An inconspicuous decoration
> made of sombre cloth, meant
> I think to be a flower, was
> pinned flat to her
> > right
> breast—any woman might have
> done the same to
> say she was a woman and warn
> us of her mood. Otherwise
> she was dressed in male attire,
> as much as to say to hell
> with you
>
> I'll speak to you, alas
> too late! ask
> What are you doing on the
> streets of Paterson? a
> thousand questions:
> Are you married? . . .
> have you read anything that I have written?
> It is all for you.

Assigning the role of sexually ambiguous Tiresias to a figure of his prospective readers rather than to himself, Williams intensified Eliot's suggestion in *The Waste Land* that it is readers who are ultimately responsible for generating reconstructive dialogue from the duplicities of modern urban experience.

We are even better prepared to mediate conflicts between one and other prescribed by patriarchal Scripture when "Paterson" plays spectator to a more

disturbing incarnation of ambiguity: a virgin/whore-spectator in the Unicorn
tapestries at the Cloisters Museum in Manhattan.

> —a fragment of the tapestry
> preserved on an end wall
>   presents a young woman
>   with rounded brow
> lost in the woods (or hiding)
>   announced . . .
>   (that it, the presentation)
> by the blowing of a hunter's horn where he stands
>   all but completely hid
>   in the leaves. She
> interests me by her singularity,
>   her courtly dress
>   among the leaves, listening!

> The expression of her face,
>   where she stands removed from the others
> —the virgin and the whore
>   an identity,
>   both for sale
> to the highest bidder!
>   and who bids higher
>   than a lover? Come
> out of it if you call yourself a woman.

The pictured virgin/whore is a more provocative emblem of a mutual exchange
of performer- and spectator-roles than the three other sexually ambiguous figures:
"Corydon," the drowned student, and the woman on the streets of Paterson.
Because the girl in the tapestry is an interpreter who cannot herself be interpreted,
she provokes the poet to challenge her in turn; he dares her to step out of the
tapestry into the hermeneutic space which his verbal work projects. But if she is
to step out of the tapestry through the text into the space in which we read it,
we are to step into the textual weave and help remake modern Paterson in the
image of an unorthodox medieval wedding-festival.

> A flight of birds, all together
> seeking their nests in the season
> a flock before dawn, small birds
> "that slepen al the night with open ye,"
> moved by desire, passionately, they

> have come a long way, commonly . . .
>   . . . the old man's mind is stirred . . .
> Their presence in the air again
> calms him. Though he is approaching
> death he is possessed by many poems . . .
>   They draw him imperiously
> to witness them . . .
>   to refresh himself
> at the sight direct from the 12th
> century what the old women or the young
> or men or boys wielding their needles . . .
> together as the cartoon has plotted it
> for them. All together, working together,
> all the birds together.

This description of picturing and pictured groups of both sexes recalls the General Prologue of Chaucer's *Canterbury Tales*, the most familiar medieval representation of communal art. But the modern poet must exaggerate the medieval poet's interest in the interplay between the subjects and objects of interpretation if he is to establish the Unicorn tapestries as images of both Paterson and *Paterson* that can help us mediate conflicts which threaten their respective integrities.

By displacing interest from the unique performer, the Unicorn, to an ambiguous spectator, the virgin/whore, Williams to some extent legitimized his prophecy of renewed communal dialogue. Reading a medieval image of community produced *by* a community, Williams's speaker sees in one figure complementary aspects of the obsession with ownership which has corrupted Paterson and could flaw the text named for the city: the virginal ideal of individual self-sufficiency and the whorish mutual exploitation. In the virgin/whore who stands removed from the others, Williams represented the ambiguities of modern life more provocatively than he did in pairing the exhibitionist Sam Patch and the introspective Mrs. Cummings. And he thus more urgently challenged us to help transform sterile opposition into productive dialogue. If we too applaud the "working together, all together" pictured in two mutually reflecting negative images of the modern city, the Unicorn tapestries and *Paterson*, we in fact already constitute a community equivalent to the one projected by the many double negations and reversals in Revelation. When Williams used the exchange between performer and witness in a European tapestry as model for the many tensions between writer and readers which animate *Paterson*, he made it clear that the place of reconstruction is not Paterson itself and not even the poem named for the city. He located renaissance in conflict between text and readers which *Paterson* generates not only by calling attention to differences between geo-history and literature but also by representing several attempts to bridge the gaps between original and image.

Book V acknowledges that *Paterson* is as much a "world of speculation" as any of Eliot's reflections upon geographic places in *Four Quartets*. The last completed book of the poem holds up a dark allegorical mirror to the four earlier books' attempts to "say it! no ideas but in things."

> —the hunt of
>> the Unicorn and
>>> the god of love
> of virgin birth
> —shall we speak of love
>> seen only in a mirror
>>> —no replica?
> reflecting only her impalpable spirit
>> which is she whom I see
>>> and not touch her flesh?

Eliot began his exploration of mortal temporality by acknowledging that poetry is generated in the no man's land between text and reader: "my words echo thus in your mind" ("Burnt Norton" I). Williams ended his attempt to transform Paterson into a new Jerusalem by acknowledging that an apocalyptic wedding can seem to take place *because* the artist — like the Unicorn — has "no mate . . . no peer" except the reader whom he sees in the mirror of his self-reflexive text.

"Shall we speak of love / seen only in a mirror?" In poetry we can *only* speak of love seen in a mirror: love seen but never to be touched. Williams therefore could achieve a reply to Greek and Latin with the bare hands by betraying the mission of the American bard as proclaimed in "Song of Myself": by using twelfth-century European artworks as mirrors of both Paterson and *Paterson* and defining the Unicorn as an apotheosis of "Paterson" (Sam Patch) who resembles Mallarmé's St. John far more than the King-self Walt Whitman.

The reality to which *Paterson* finally points is alien to the American marketplace and *thus* capable of finding ideas in its things.

> A WORLD OF ART
> THAT THROUGH THE YEARS HAS
> *SURVIVED*!

> —the museum become real
> *The Cloisters*
> on its rock

> casting its shadow—
>   "la réalité! la réalité!
>   la réa! la réa! la réalité!"

As the Unicorn is French—French or Flemish, says Williams, trying to interweave the Unicorn-crucifixion with the Breughel *Nativity*—"*the Cloisters* / on its rock / casting its shadow" becomes real only in the form of a self-echoing exclamation in French. Similarly, Williams domesticated the regal foreign Unicorn by reporting that it has been seen on the American plains by a regal French explorer/ artist:

> Audubon (Au-du-bon), (the lost Dauphin)
>   left the boat
>   downstream
> below the falls of the Ohio at Louisville
>   to follow
> a trail through the woods
>   across three states
>   northward of Kentucky
> He saw buffalo
>   and more
>   a horned beast among the trees
> in the moonlight
>   following small birds
> the chicadee
>   in a field crowded with small flowers
>   its neck
>   circled by a crown!
>   from a regal tapestry of
>   stars!

Like all early travellers in the New World, an aristocratic Frenchman would naturally make the wilderness his mirror and translate American nature into the civilized terms of traditional fables—thus anticipating in reverse Eliot's prescription of interplay between each American individual talent and the Mind of Europe. Williams had to stress the fact that vision is intersubjective in order to construct a "temple" which is not threatened but animated by the continual loss of sense in the fall and flow of language as well as time.

> that the poem the most perfect rock and temple, the highest
> falls, in clouds of gauzy spray, should be so rivaled . . . that the poet

in disgrace, should borrow from erudition (to unslave the mind): rail-
ing at the vocabulary (borrowing from those he hates, to his own
disenfranchisement)

It is because Williams consistently looked to Tradition for paradoxical readings
of loss as gain that he could rival the complex idea of a reconciliation of form
and flux which he found in the things of Paterson, its architecture, and its falls.

Williams finally countered the fact that what passes for common sense in
America is a mechanical recycling of worn-out conventions—"the ignorant sun /
rising in the slot / of hollow suns risen"—by having his speaker read a medieval
visual narrative of apocalyptic challenge and marriage as model for the genesis
of community from violent questionings of individual identity. Associating himself with the obviously artificial, non-American museum-Unicorn, "Paterson"
can make the fundamental problem of the American artist the ground of its
resolution:

> Here
> is not there,
> and will never be.
> The Unicorn
> has no match
> or mate   the artist
> has no peer
> Death
> has no peer:
> wandering in the woods,
> a field crowded with small flowers
> in which the wounded beast lies down to rest

> We shall not get to the bottom:
> death is a hole
> in which we are all buried
> Gentile and Jew.

> The flower dies down
> and rots away
> But there is a hole
> in the bottom of the bag

> It is the imagination
> which cannot be fathomed.
> It is through this hole
> we escape

So through art alone, male and female, a field of
flowers, a tapestry, spring flowers unequaled
in loveliness
    Through this hole
    at the bottom of the cavern
    of death, the imagination
    escapes intact.

he bears a collar round his neck
    hid in bristling hair

"Divorce is / the sign of knowledge in our time, / divorce! divorce!" There is really no way of marrying here and there, Paterson and the Cloisters, America and Europe, life and art, life and death—readers and poet. Yet as we are all to be buried in death, both Gentile and Jew ("Gentile or Jew . . . consider Phlebas, who was once handsome and tall as you," *The Waste Land* IV), Williams's catalogue of divorces may project a common immortality even more authoritatively than Stevens's evocation of a ring of men who perish but sing to the sun. "There is a hole in the bottom of the bag . . . it is through this hole we escape." For Williams, imagination is not the constructive, esemplastic power it is for Coleridge: it is negative and *dis*integrative. As we have seen, Book V of *Paterson* mirrors both the city Paterson and itself in the tapestries that hang in a building which is in turn mirrored by the Hudson if seen from the New Jersey—the Paterson—side of the river, and reality becomes no more than shadows of images articulated in a foreign language: "la réa, la réa, la réalité." But if the Unicorn's impotent solitude reminds us that Williams's attempt to build a New Jerusalem will inevitably fail, we can redefine our common mortality—of which the immortalizing museum is the lifeless counterpart—as the principle of true community.

A macabre visualization of the conflict evoked by the phrase "Gentile and Jew" helps us reflect upon a bewildering series of mirrorings in ways that project an equivalent of the templeless City in Revelation. The speaker remembers a distinctly untraditional avatar of the self-sacrificing Lamb-Unicorn "Paterson": one whom no temple, museum or library can fully domesticate.

    I . . .   laughed
recalling the Jew
    in the pit
        among his fellows
when the indifferent gun
        was spraying the heap
he had not yet been hit
but smiled

> comforting his companions
>   comforting
>   his companions

The gently smiling Unicorn matches the anonymous dying Jew, and both match not only the *Paterson*-poet and "Paterson," his chief persona, but also—potentially—Paterson itself. Initiating endless interplay among these correspondences, the text challenges us to make the museum real and to make the Spirit and the Bride Jerusalem invite us all to a wedding-supper—just as "Little Gidding" challenges us to conspire with the poet in renewing Pentecost by outrageously equating the Nazi dive-bomber with the Spirit ("the dark dove with the flickering tongue . . . the dove descending breaks the air / With flame of incandescent terror").

Literary art can never be adequately defined because like "la réalité" it is both intertextual and intersubjective.

> A flight of birds, all together,
> seeking their nests in the season
> a flock before dawn, small birds
> "That slepen al the night with open ye,"
> moved by desire, passionately, they
> have come a long way, commonly.
> Now they separate and go by pairs
> each to his appointed mating. The
> colors of their plumage are undecipherable
> in the sun's glare against the sky
> but the old man's mind is stirred
> by the white, the yellow, the black
> as if he could see them there.

Isolated subjectivity can animate intersubjective community, however, if mental reflection ("the mind is the demon / drives us") is matched by self-reflexive representations of itself: by works such as *Paterson* and the Unicorn tapestries which associate art and the communal scattering of identity in ritual sacrifice.

Certainly art imitates our possession by demonic dreams.

> Dreams possess me
>   and the dance
>   of my thoughts
> involving animals
>   the blameless beasts
>
> .   .   .   .

> Though he is approaching
> death he is possessed by many poems.

But artistic play differs from the dream-work in that it occurs *between* subjects
—"my words echo thus in your mind" Eliot said—and is composed not of ideas
but things: words, paint, threads. The Unicorn-like pure reality which can cure
the corruption of Paterson, N.J., comes from the materials of art, not from some
transcendent Platonic realm of ideas.

> Pollock's blobs of paint squeezed out
> with design!
> pure from the tube. Nothing else
> is real

> The Unicorn roams the forest of all true
> lovers' minds. They hunt it down. Bow wow!
> sing hey the green holly!

> —every married man carries in his head
> the beloved and sacred image
> of a virgin
> whom he has whored
> but the living fiction
> a tapestry
> silk and wool shot with silver threads
> a milk-white one-horned beast

Of course the Unicorn is an image reflected in as many minds as are activated by
desire ("roams the forest of all true lovers' minds"). But that desire is to be
articulated by objective, material prefigurations of wholeness ("the living fiction /
a tapestry / silk and wool shot with silver threads").

Yet such an objective prefiguration of mental reflection can allow the museum to become real only because it is an image *of* witnessing. "In a field with
small flowers / its neck circled by a crown / from a regal tapestry of stars" the
Unicorn is chiefly characterized by his own visible, gentle eye, as regal as the
"Dauphin" Audubon, witness to a New World:

> lying wounded on his belly
> legs folded under him
> the bearded head held
> regally aloft

As the four living creatures seen across the sea of glass in Revelation prefigure the
perfect, foursquare City because they have eyes within and all around, the silver,

silk and wool Unicorn in the Cloisters tapestries reflects his counterpart across
the actual sea in the Musée de Cluny: the beast who is captured by the Lady
when he is reflected in her mirror.

> —shall we speak of love
>> seen only in a mirror
>>> —no replica?
>> reflecting only her impalpable spirit?
>> which is she whom I see
>>> and not touch her flesh?

"Paterson's" totemic image thus generates not only recollection of intensely visible
destruction—in effect a blinding—but also of a thrusting *counter*-sign to his
fallen horn.

> silk and wool shot with silver threads
>> a milk-white one horned beast
>>> I, Paterson, the King-self
> saw the lady
>> through the rough woods
>>> outside the palace walls
> among the stench of sweating horses
>> and gored hounds
>>> yelping with pain
> the heavy breathing pack
>> to see the dead beast
>>> brought in at last
> across the saddlebow
>> among the oak trees.
>> Paterson,
> keep your pecker up
>> whatever the detail!

The elaborate display of the Unicorn's regal impotence makes regal "Paterson"
potent. For like *Paterson* as well as the highly concentrated first-person account
of sacrifice in Mallarmé's "Cantique de St. Jean" it makes its interpreters undergo
the potentially creative alienation of self-criticism.

STEPHEN CUSHMAN

The World Is Not Iambic:
Measure as Trope

We do not live in a sonnet world; we do not live even in an iambic world;
certainly not in a world of iambic pentameters.

—"VS" (1948)

Exploring Williams's theory of measure entails a certain amount of deciphering, translating, and filling in of blanks. Here is what Williams says his verse is doing, and here is what it actually does. Can the two be reconciled? They can, but the reconciliation requires first solving some basic problems in Williams's terminology. [Problems in terminology that have to do with formal schemes have been discussed elsewhere.] Lineation, enjambment, caesurae, and typographic design all are matters of the surface patterning of verse. This [essay] turns from a discussion of measure-as-scheme to the consideration of measure-as-trope. If Williams is using "measure" figuratively, what is it a figure of? Although several passages in his critical prose might provide starting points, I shall begin by looking to the Theatre of Trope, the poems themselves.

In "The Desert Music" (1951), a poem that combines autobiography with poetic creed, Williams considers measure at the outset:

> How shall we get said what must be said?
>
> Only the poem.
> Only the counted poem, to an exact measure:
> to imitate, not to copy nature, not
> to copy nature

From *William Carlos Williams and the Meaning of Measure*. © 1985 by Yale University. Yale University Press, 1985. Originally entitled "The World Is Not Iambic."

> NOT, prostrate, to copy nature
>   but a dance! to dance
>   two and two with him —
>   sequestered there asleep,
>   right end up!

In the insistence on counting we hear the familiar rhetoric of formal scheme. For him, Williams claims, getting said what must be said necessarily involves poetry, and poetry necessarily involves verse organized in some numerical mode, because no verse is free. But although we may be tempted to take this statement at face value, the verse scheme subverts that statement, establishing an early irony in the poem. "The Desert Music" opens with a regular iambic pentameter line:

> —the dánce begíns: to end abóut a fórm

If a "counted poem," that is, a metrical one, is the proper medium for getting said what he must say, then all Williams has to do is keep churning out stacks of iambic pentameter lines. But the counted poem is not the proper medium, and the first few lines of "The Desert Music" enact the rejection of a metrical scheme. In its quest "to end about a form," meaning both a poetic form and the form propped motionless on the International Bridge between Juárez and El Paso, the poem begins by invoking and then departing from the dominant scheme of its tradition. In its place "The Desert Music" establishes the conventions of line-sentence counterpointing, which are measured out against the standard of the one-sentence, noncaesural line "How shall we get said what must be said?"

Even though Williams's insistence on a countable scheme must be approached cautiously, the phrase "an exact measure" does seem to have a meaning that transcends the specific, technical features of versification. Having asserted that getting said what must be said involves the poem, and the poem involves "an exact measure," Williams establishes a metonymic relation between how the poem says what must be said and the idea of measuring. With the added qualification "to imitate, not to copy nature, not / to copy nature," the meaning of the metonymy emerges. How shall we get said what must be said? By means of measuring what we must say with imitation. Although formal scheme will inevitably figure in the mimetic project, it is only a part of that project. Many misreadings of Williams, as well as some of his own confusions, originate here, in the inference that he is saying reductively, the way to make poems that say something is to invent a nonmetrical formal scheme based on pseudo-quantitative theory.

In "The Desert Music," then, measure is a trope of mimesis, the poetic mode Williams deems most appropriate and effective for getting said what must be said; to imitate is to measure. Using "measure" this way, he taps the etymological meaning "to be meet," that is, commensurate, fitting, or appropriate. In the course of the poem, the embodiment of this mimetic measuring appears in the person of the "worn-out trouper from the states," a stripper dancing in a bar south of the border. The description of her gyrates through five neatly symmetric quatrains before yielding to the asymmetry of verse paragraphing, the typographic format Williams reserves for a shift in tone:

> What the hell
> are you grinning
> to yourself about? Not
> at *her?*
> The music!
> I like her. She fits
>
> the music

The final typographic isolation of "the music" extricates this phrase from its immediate literal context and associates it with the figurative music of the desert. She fits, or measures, both the actual music she is dancing to, a striptease played "perfunc- / torily" by a "conventional orchestra," and an "insensate" music in the mind, an organizing aesthetic principle which the mind projects onto fragments of experience and perception. She is, for Williams, the emblem of mimesis. Stripped of covering fictions and illusions, the bored, exhausted dancer confronts us with the pathetic shabbiness of an imaginative desert; and yet "There is a fascination / seeing her shake" as "One is moved but not / at the dull show." What is fascinating and moving about her is the "grace of / a certain candor," which she retains by not pretending to be anything more or less than she is. In the same way, the poem gets said what must be said: that out of the barrenness of reality, "the dull show," comes the material to be shaped candidly into an aesthetic configuration.

The association of measurement with imitation in "The Desert Music" represents a single instance of a discussion that runs through letters, essays, and other poems. The authority to whom Williams refers throughout this discussion is Aristotle, particularly the Aristotle of the *Poetics*. As with other authorities he cites, however, the boundary between what comes from Aristotle and what comes from Williams's understanding of Aristotle is not always clear. While writing "The Desert Music," Williams told Kenneth Burke that recently he had come to understand the real "significance of Aristotle's use of the word 'imitation.' " He then moves to the formulation found in "The Desert Music":

> The imagination has to imitate nature, not to copy it — as the famous speech in *Hamlet* has led us to believe. There is a world of difference there. The whole dynamic of the art approach is involved, to imitate invokes the verb, to copy invokes nothing but imbecility. It is the very essence of the difference between realism and cubism with everything in favor of the latter.

Whereas the distinction between imitating and copying may be implicit in Aristotle's *Poetics*, as Aristotle revises Plato's disparaging view that mimesis involves merely counterfeiting external appearances (*Republic*, Book Ten), Williams's formulation here owes more to Coleridge. In all imitation, Coleridge argues, two elements must coexist: likeness and unlikeness, or sameness and difference. In a genuine imitation there must be "likeness in the difference, difference in the likeness, and a reconcilement of both in one." If there is only likeness to nature "without any check of difference," then the would-be imitator has produced a mere copy, so that "the result is disgusting, and the more complete the delusion, the more loathsome the effect." Returning to Williams's example of the difference between realism and cubism "with everything in favor of the latter," we infer that, for him, the superior mimetic power of cubism originates in its combination of a recognizable likeness to reality with a radical difference from it.

Although he claims to grasp the real significance of Aristotle's word "imitation," Williams does not, for example, wrestle out the implications for modern lyric poetry of a theory concerned primarily with tragic action or epic narrative. Although he might have, he does not locate in Aristotle's discussion of plots a sanction for his own conception of poetic structure. Instead, Williams's borrowings from Aristotle are selective. One aspect of the *Poetics* he apparently found attractive is its discussion of prosodic matters. Mariani states that in 1937 Williams suggested to Zukofsky that they collaborate on a book about modern prosody which would begin with Aristotle. In the language and argument of this passage from the twenty-fourth chapter of the *Poetics* appear formulations Williams might have enlisted in his cause:

> As for the meter, the heroic measure has proved its fitness by the test of experience. If a narrative poem in any other meter or in many meters were now composed, it would be found incongruous. For of all measures the heroic is the stateliest and the most massive; and hence it most readily admits rare words and metaphors, which is another point in which the narrative form of imitation stands alone. On the other hand, the iambic and the trochaic tetrameter are stirring measures, the latter being akin to dancing, the former expressive of action. Still more absurd would it be to mix together different meters, as was done by Chaeremon. Hence no one has ever composed a poem

on a great scale in any other than heroic verse. Nature herself, as we
have said, teaches the choice of the proper measure.

"Nature herself . . . teaches the choice of the proper measure." Lifted from its
immediate context, this statement could easily serve as the slogan for several versions of mimetic or organic theory, as it confers on formal scheme—in this case,
heroic measure—mimetic power. In rendering his translation of Aristotle, S. H.
Butcher uses "measure" in two different ways. First, he uses it specifically in
the phrase "heroic measure" (*hērōikon*) as a synonym for "meter," having used
"meter" to translate the Greek *metron*. But, second, in the final sentence of the
passage he chooses "proper measure" for *harmotton*, accusative form of a noun
derived from the verb *harmozō*, which means "to fit well," "to suit," "to be
adapted for," or "to be in tune." Williams read Butcher's translation, published
in 1932, at the Gratwick farm in July 1949. Butcher's double use of "measure"
accurately reflects the basic Aristotelian notion that in a poetic imitation measurement takes place at two levels. Here Aristotle insists on a relation between these
levels, asserting the fitness of a particular meter for epic poetry, which he calls
"the narrative form of imitation." In arguing for this fitness, he links the prosodic
measurement of verse scheme to the mimetic measurement of narrative poetry.

Although the linking of verse measurement to mimetic measurement might
seem obvious to anyone, like Williams, who leans toward an organic theory of
poetic form, Aristotle's assertion that Nature (*physis*) teaches the choice of the
proper measure can be misunderstood out of context. Construed one way, it could
mean that there must be a natural, or organic, relation between verse measurement and mimetic measurement, the kind of relation, Williams argues, only
nonmetrical verse can provide. But, as the rest of the passage shows, this is not at
all what Aristotle has in mind. For him the "natural" relation of meter to matter
is not organic, at least in any sense that American poets since Whitman would
understand; it is highly conventional, with poetic conventions based on the fitness
of a particular meter for a particular matter: heroic for epic narrative, iambic for
action, trochaic for dancing. In the case of heroic meter, for example, its appropriateness for epic poetry rests not on anything inherently dactylic in the adventures of Odysseus, but on the ease with which dactylic meter accommodates the
"rare words and metaphors" Homer uses to describe those adventures. There is,
however, nothing inevitable or necessary about the relation of dactylic meter to
the subjects of epic narrative; that relation arises from literary custom or usage,
Aristotle's "test of experience."

This subtlety may have escaped Williams altogether, or he may have chosen
to ignore it. At any rate, he does assume a necessary relation between verse measurement and mimetic measurement, as seen in the unfinished essay "Measure"
(1959): "What I in my American world am proposing is that they divide their

lines differently and see what comes of it. We are finished with the aberration of free verse, but we have to learn to recount, taking our idiom as a constant (and for that we have to know what we are talking) and make units of it which we compose into our effects." The mimetic nature of lyric poetry differs from that of epic or dramatic, because the lyric poem does not imitate events or actions. Instead, it imitates speech, or "ahistorical utterance." According to Williams, the speech of Americans constitutes an idiom that is distinct from British English. Therefore, Williams implies, lyric poems which purport to imitate American speech must break with the conventions of English prosody. In the passage above he recommends that American poets "divide their lines differently and see what comes of it." What Williams hopes will come of it is that American poets, in taking "our idiom as a constant," will make prosodic units ("variable feet") out of linguistic patterns and contours. Here Williams makes the mistake of confusing the object imitated (an American idiom) with the design of the mimetic medium (nonmetrical verse patterns), which—because an imitation is a trope of the object imitated—is a confusion of trope and scheme. In fact, what Williams gets when he divides his lines "differently" is enjambment, and the relation of enjambed verse to American speech is just as arbitrary and, by now, conventional as the relation of dactylic meter to the adventures of epic heroes. Certainly there is nothing inherently or necessarily enjambment-like in the way Americans express themselves with words.

Although Williams may not do justice to the complexities of Aristotelian mimesis, he does appropriate the Aristotelian idiom in expanding his concept of measure to include the act of imitation itself. Outside Williams's critical prose, measure and measuring appear most often as figurations of mimesis in *Paterson*, which is not surprising, for, like "The Desert Music," *Paterson* meditates extensively on the nature of poetry and the poetic project. As in "The Desert Music," this meditation accompanies a wide display of verse schemes, giving those schemes a peculiar self-reflexive status. They serve Williams not only as the media for his imitation, but also, in moments when *Paterson* contemplates itself, as self-conscious examples of their own mimetic power. Beyond these immediate similarities to "The Desert Music," however, lie the unique features of *Paterson* as a long poem in the American tradition that descends from Whitman's "Song of Myself" and includes the long poems of Eliot, Crane, Stevens, Pound, Zukofsky, and Olson. As a long poem, *Paterson* must confront the problems of its own form, working to create an imitation of the heterogeneous man-city, while also contending with its own formal heterogeneity. How can *Paterson* fashion unity out of such diversity? This is its major theme.

In making both its mimetic and its prosodic measurements, the long poem must avoid disintegrating into a sequence of fragments. A showcase of verse forms, *Paterson* struggles continually with its own fragmentation. Punctuated with prose interludes, the formal surface of the poem is also fractured repeatedly by shifts among various verse arrangements: long lines, short lines, verse paragraphs, unrhymed couplets, tercets, quatrains, triadic stanzas, sapphics, and short rhymed songs. Occasionally ghosts of an iambic pentameter appear to recall a superseded order, as in "The province of the poem is the world" or "What end but love, that stares death in the eye?" Operating throughout the poem are the conventions of line-sentence counterpointing and typographic inscription, both symmetric and asymmetric. Lines are fragmented, pages are fragmented, sections are fragmented. Even the poem itself is a fragment, for, with a sixth book projected, it remains unfinished. Against the threat of so much disorder Williams's immediate defense is the three-part structure he builds into each of the five books. Like the triadic stanza, the three-part structure landscapes its material with a recognizable, predictable measure. A numerical mode of organization, the three-part structure provides each book and the poem as a whole with a controlling "meter."

Williams's second defense against the threat of his long poem disintegrating into fragments—or rather, against the charge that it does so—is to explore the relation of verse measurement to mimetic measurement as a theme in the poem itself, implicitly arguing for the appropriateness of his form. To the end of Book One he appends a quotation from John Addington Symonds's *Studies of the Greek Poets* (1880):

> N.B. "In order apparently to bring the meter still more within the sphere of prose and common speech, Hipponax ended his iambics with a spondee or a trochee instead of an iambus, doing thus the utmost violence to the rhythmical structure. These deformed and mutilated verses were called [choliambi] (lame or limping iambics). They communicated a curious crustiness to the style. The choliambi are in poetry what the dwarf or cripple is in human nature. Here again, by their acceptance of this halting meter, the Greeks displayed their acute aesthetic sense of propriety, recognizing the harmony which subsists between crabbed verses and the distorted subjects with which they dealt—the vices and perversions of humanity—as well as their agreement with the snarling spirit of the satirist. Deformed verse was suited to deformed morality."

As with any of the other prose sections of *Paterson*, we wonder how to read this quotation. Is it indeed an explanatory note to take at face value? Or, as with many of Eliot's notes to *The Waste Land*, should we be on guard against irony and evasion? The safest answer is "Both." At the outset of *Paterson* Williams announces that his poem is "a reply to Greek and Latin with the bare hands," an attempt to fashion out of modern American life and speech a poem worthy of inclusion in an epic tradition. Against the background of this announcement, a direct invocation of classical models arouses suspicion that Williams is perhaps patronizing the university scholar and his love of Greek, Latin, libraries, and footnotes. At the same time, however, *Paterson* shows again and again that replying to the classical tradition involves bringing ancient forms into the modern poem in order to renovate them for use in the present, whether it be the stanza of Sappho, the idyll of Theocritus, or the dance of the satyr.

Given that Williams's quotation of Symonds should be approached with caution, the passage is a full and suggestive one. In the poetry of Hipponax Williams finds a model for doing the utmost violence to metrical structure in order to bring his measure into the sphere of prose and common speech. By suggesting an analogy between ancient poetic practice and his own project, Williams anticipates the objection that poetry which makes use of prose rhythms is in fact not poetry at all. Beyond this simple analogy, however, lies Williams's tacit acceptance of a theory of poetic form that sees in the relation of verse scheme to mimetic trope an underlying "harmony" and "propriety." A certain kind of verse is "suited to" a certain kind of subject matter.

Clearly, Aristotle's notion of the fitness of the proper measure hovers behind Symonds's terminology, as it does behind Williams's etymological sense of measurement as meting out, or allotment according to what is meet, fitting, or proper. But the passage from Symonds is more than a mandate for verse schemes that are mimetically appropriate. After all, many a passage from Aristotle could provide Williams with that. More important, in the context of *Paterson*, this passage points to a particular kind of verse and subject matter combined in the poetry of Hipponax. Symonds describes the lame or halting verses of Hipponax as being to poetry "what the dwarf or cripple is in human nature." When distorted subjects, such as the vices and perversions of humanity, are under scrutiny, mutilated, crabbed verses, which range freely into prose and common speech, are in order. That Williams took this truth to heart is clear from a letter he wrote John Holmes six years after the publication of Book One:

> What shall we say more of the verse that is to be left behind by the age we live in if it does not have some of the marks the age has made upon us, its poets? The traumas of today, God knows, are plain enough upon our minds. Then how shall our poems escape? They should be horrible things, those poems. To the classic muse their bodies should appear to be covered with sores. They should be hunchbacked, limping. And yet our poems must show how we have struggled with them to measure and control them. And we must SUCCEED even while we succumb.

Williams's graphic language describes the poems of the modern age as maimed, monstrous creations embodying terrible knowledge; and yet, for all their monstrosity, these poems are meted out appropriately to the monstrous world they imitate. Hunchbacked, limping verse suits a long poem about, among other things, the way men and women behave and misbehave in an age marked by historical trauma and psychological fragmentation; but the example of Hipponax, as Symonds interprets it, has other implications. Hunchbacked, limping verse also suits "the snarling spirit of the satirist," who employs derision, irony, and wit to expose and criticize the deformed morality of our vices and perversions. As a poet Williams is only sometimes a satirist, and as a satirist he is only sometimes a snarling one. Still, his quotation of Symonds implies a recognition that the fragmented body of *Paterson* suits not only its subject matter, but also his own attitude toward the deformities of the man-city.

The always implicit and sometimes explicit argument of *Paterson*, then, is that its verse schemes suit its imitation of the world. To those who charge that the apparent fragmentation and overall formlessness of the poem render it a literary failure, Williams's answer, I infer, would be that they have missed the point: the poem is fragmented and apparently formless because it imitates the world, and the world is often fragmented and apparently formless. In *A Novelette* (1932), Williams comments on the fragmented technique of *Kora in Hell*, defending its "shifting of category" against Pound's anticipated criticisms. The shifting of category accounts, in Williams's view, for the "excellence" of his improvisations: "It is the disjointing process." Setting aside the possible counterargument that an imitation of fragmentation and formlessness is not necessarily rendered successful by being fragmented and formless, we might take Williams at his word and read certain passages of *Paterson* as further examples that measurement is simply a metaphor for mimesis. These readings would find support in Williams's earnest declaration that "not until I have made of it a replica / will my sins be forgiven and my / disease cured." Here Williams ascribes to his poem not only the mimetic status of a literary work, but also the supramimetic healing power of an icon or idol. Suddenly, the poetic act of imitation assumes a spiritual significance, which in turn may account for much of the missionary zeal behind Williams's crusade for the theory of measure.

The problem is that when Williams uses "measure" figuratively, it is not always as a simple figure of mimesis. Even though the mimetic meaning of measure is the one he recognizes and insists on, it is not always the meaning that particular passages and contexts point to. Furthermore, this same insistence sometimes leads him to make overly reductive statements about mimetic measurement, statements which interpret that measurement too narrowly, such as this one published in 1948, the same year as *Paterson*, Book Two:

> Look! the fixed overall quality of all poems of the past was a plainly
> understandable counting. The lines were measured and in general
> evenly arranged—to reveal a similar orderliness of thought and be-
> havior in the general pattern of their day. Such measures (notice the
> word) were synonymous with a society, uniform, and made up of
> easily measurable integers, racial and philosophical.
>
>   . . . Thus there was a correlation between the world as it stood
> politically and philosophically and the form of the poem that repre-
> sented it—noticeably so in Dante's terza rima.
>
>   . . . We do not live in a sonnet world; we do not live even in an
> iambic world; certainly not in a world of iambic pentameters.

Whereas the assumption that "there was a correlation between the world as it
stood politically and philosophically and the form of the poem that represented
it" is reasonable enough, Williams overstates that correlative relation in order to
challenge the assumption of Eliot's "Tradition and the Individual Talent" (1919).
Rejected here is a recognition of the fundamentally conventional and traditional
nature of verse schemes and poetic imitations. Certainly, a poet's attitude toward
poetic form will reflect a larger attitude toward "an orderliness of thought and
behavior," which in turn may even reflect a larger cultural ethos. As Williams
argues in "Against the Weather" (1939), "Dante fastened upon his passion a
whole hierarchy of formal beliefs . . . facing a time and place and enforcement
which were his 'weather.' " By casting his verse in *terza rima*, Dante revealed his
attitude toward the theological and philosophical systems of his day: "The dogmatist in Dante chose a triple multiple for his poem, the craftsman skilfully followed orders—but the artist?"

But if poetic form reflects historical reality, the reality reflected is also that
of literary history, not just political. The sonnet may have come into English
poetic tradition at a particular moment, but that does not make it the sole prop-
erty of that historical moment. The dogmatist in Williams, who seems to use
polemical statements to jolt the reader out of intellectual complacency, wants to
deny the historical continuity of culture in order to affirm its discontinuity,
which, as Daniel Hoffman argues, "makes each moment, each act, each emotion
experientially unique and therefore requires that style and form be provisional,
experimental, reflective of the process of becoming self-aware rather than of the
continuation of any familiar category of expression, thought, or feeling." Once
again Williams confronts us with a metonymy that collapses the series of complex links between a culture and its verse. By arguing that measures are "synonymous" with particular moments in social and political history, he not only re-
duces the mimetic function of those measures to a crude, historically determined
mirroring; he also evades the meanings of measure which point back to him. . . .

"Measure serves for us as the key." In context Williams means by this that the measurements we make between objects confirm their existence. Although as an epistemological proposition this statement vexes with its incompleteness, as a proposition about the aesthetic theory of William Carlos Williams it radiates a truth which its immediate context cannot contain. Measure serves Williams as the key to many of the questions poetry raises. As a prosodic term, it addresses the question, What is the nature of the modern verse scheme? As an aesthetic concept, it addresses the question, What is the nature of the modern mimetic project? As a richly expressive metaphor, it addresses the question, What are the psychological and emotional needs of modern men and women? As "measure" slides along a spectrum of meanings from scheme towards trope, denotation towards connotation, it allows Williams to examine the various relationships a poem maintains: poem to language, poem to world, poem to reader, poem to poet.

One [other relationship remains]: that of a poem to other poets, or poem to tradition. Of all the ways in which measure serves Williams as the key, this one has an importance that cannot be overestimated. For him measure serves as the key to the tradition, enabling him to confront the poets who, for various reasons, matter most. A full generation after Williams's death, his critics and admirers may argue that his poetry alone would have placed him squarely within the tradition, which may or may not be true. But, true or false, it is not the point; the point is that for Williams measure provided a sense of poetic mission. It gave him an ideological platform on which to build a campaign. Upon that platform measure secured itself a meaning which, no matter how much he preached and theorized, Williams could never exhaust.

Williams's theory of measure grew, in part, out of his response to Whitman. Poe's idea of quantity provided Williams with theoretical sponsorship, which allowed him to circumvent Whitman, while claiming kinship with an earlier poet in his own tradition. But the theory of measure reflects Williams's confrontations with other poets as well. Twenty-two years after Eliot made his pronouncement on the subject, Williams took up the problem of tradition and the individual talent in a recently published essay, written in either later 1941 or early 1942, "Let Us Order Our World":

> He who will write the first ranking verse of his day will be he who
> expands the tradition to a point sufficient to bear the heaviest strains
> put upon it by the demands of the day without breaking down. That
> is, not only the style of the structural devices employed must be ade-
> quate to the strain they are expected to bear. New devices are neces-
> sary. You cannot fly through the clouds in a coach and four though
> the purpose remains the same, to arrive safely at the end of a journey:

partly so, for there are today reaches of the understanding that were unattainable except to the imagination of former times.

On the surface Williams's approach to tradition has little in common with Eliot's discussion of the shred of platinum analogous to a poet's mind, the escape from emotion, or the extinction of personality; yet this passage does reveal Williams's underlying commitment to what Eliot calls "the historical sense," rather than to the antihistorical discontinuity which surfaces in his remarks about Dante in "VS," published six or seven years later. Writing "first ranking verse" necessitates expanding the tradition, and typically Williams argues that, in order to expand the tradition, a poet must invent new "structural devices." Behind this phrase lies an allusion to, among other things, the new measurements of formal schemes. Shifting to an analogy of his own, Williams then turns to the inadequacy of a horse-drawn coach in circumstances that require an airplane. As usual, Williams masks his historical sense of literature with a metaphor which implies that poetry must make new discoveries and inventions the way science and technology have.

In the next paragraph the flying analogy reappears, but with a new perspective on expanding the tradition:

> Thus the complexity of modern thought, for one thing involving a complete change of base, often, as compared with former concepts, goes on increasing. And whereas all solutions are alike in beauty and simplicity when attained, the means to attain them will today involve enormous excursions of inventive skill before the answers can be brought home. Sometimes a man is flying upside down without knowing it and may be still advancing. Order is still there but you'd hardly recognize it for what it was formerly. Enterprises of the imagination must be made retroactive upon old rules which unless they permit limitless expansion cannot but be adjudged trivial or false. By release we confirm, by restraint we destroy.

An emphasis on "order" now joins the call for new structural devices. If Williams had written this essay ten or fifteen years later, he probably would have used the word "measure" instead. At any rate, we know we are on familiar ground because the notion of ordering leads directly to the dualities of limit and limitlessness, restraint and release. Here, however, Williams shrugs off the necessity of limits and restraint, calling instead for an "expanded, liberated, unrestrained tradition of verse." A different tone appears four years after "Let Us Order Our World" when Williams, struggling with *Paterson*, writes in a letter to Kenneth Burke of awaking with "a half-sentence on my metaphorical lips, 'the limitations of form.'

It seemed to mean something of importance." This suggests that at other moments Williams did not find the limitations of form so easy to shrug off. That he should feel ambivalent towards those limitations comes as no real surprise, however, for contradictions riddle his attitude toward the tradition from which he inherits them.

"Let us order our world." Perhaps revealing Williams's attitude towards World War II, it is a catchy slogan, coming from a man who enjoyed slogans in a period that generated many: the local is the universal; no ideas but in things; verse must be measured. This particular slogan is characteristic of Williams's thinking, which often recalls an Elizabethan world picture, as it fuses the microcosmic order of the poem to the macrocosmic orders of the world and universe. "Let Us Order Our World" caps a period of four or five years during which Williams turned repeatedly to the subject of order in his essays, notably in "The Basis of Faith in Art" (1937?) and "Against the Weather: A Study of the Artist" (1939). In the former, for example, Williams stages an imaginary dialogue with his brother, who accuses him of having a disorderly mind. Williams answers:

> But you mentioned something about order—you said I had a disorderly mind. If to have a mind in which order is broken down to be redistributed, then you are right, not otherwise. . . . But order is in its vigor the process of ordering—a function of the imagination—

Here Williams anticipates the self-description in "The Desert Music": "I am that he whose brains / are scattered / aimlessly." His description of the imagination as the faculty which disorders so that it can reorder recalls Coleridge's distinction between primary and secondary imaginations. Soon after this statement, in the middle of Williams's career, the concept of measure begins its dramatic expansion from prosody into mythology. This is no coincidence. In calling for order in our poems, our lives, and our world, Williams speaks out of his own beliefs and needs; yet in relying on the word "order" again and again, he finds himself tangled in the slogans of others. There was Stevens's invocation of order in *Ideas of Order* (1936), particularly in "The Idea of Order at Key West": "Oh! Blessed rage for order, pale Ramon, / the maker's rage to order words of the sea." And, besides Stevens, there was Pound, whose ideas of order may have drained the term of its usefulness for Williams.

In Pound's Canto 13, published in the *Transatlantic Review* (1924) and in his *Draft of 16 Cantos* printed in 1925, appears this passage:

> And Kung said, and wrote on the bo leaves:
> If a man have not order within him

> He can not spread order about him;
> And if a man have not order within him
> His family will not act with due order;
>   And if the prince have not order within him
> He can not put order in his dominions.
> And Kung gave the words "order"
> and "brotherly deference"
> And said nothing of the "life after death."

In this passage Pound presents a Confucian idea of order: the social order depends on and reflects the ethical and spiritual order of society's leaders and citizens. This order finds itself expressed here in verse which combines the rhetorical rhythm of Confucian aphorism with a loose triple meter; through these techniques also surface traces of Whitman, as anaphora and syntactic parallelism lend the passage the smooth elegance and balance Whitman discovered in Biblical wisdom literature. As it stands, the argument of Canto 13 seems consonant with Williams's own thinking about the relation between psychological and social order. Nevertheless, in his essay "Excerpts from a Critical Sketch: *A Draft of XXX Cantos* by Ezra Pound" (1931), Williams reveals a crucial difference between himself and Pound: "It is in the minutiae—in the minute organization of the words and their relationships in a composition that the seriousness and value of a work of writing exist—*not* in the sentiments, ideas, schemes portrayed." Implicit in the phrase "the seriousness and value of a work of writing" is a reply to Pound's essay "The Serious Artist," published in *The Egoist* in 1913, in which Pound argues that good art is art which "bears true witness," art which is most precise in its definitions of "the inner nature and conditions of man." Pound goes on to associate good writing with "perfect control" and "orderliness." Although one can easily overstate the importance of any one passage or, by singling out one cause, oversimplify a series of complex developments, Williams's reply to Pound prophesies the split between the two poets with uncanny precision. His own poetry is hardly without sentiments and ideas, but throughout his career Williams doggedly insisted on the primacy of "minutiae," on the "minute organization of the words and their relationships in a composition," whereas Pound led his *Cantos* deeper and deeper into "the sentiments, ideas, schemes portrayed." By 1935, when he published *Jefferson and/or Mussolini*, Pound's idea of order carried implications Williams found troubling: "The great man is filled with a very different passion, the will toward *order*." The will toward order in the formal schemes of verse is one thing, but Williams felt in the fascism of Mussolini quite another.

    Although Pound's ideas of order, both prosodic and social, unquestionably influenced Williams's own thinking about measure, it became imperative, for poetic and political reasons, that Williams establish some distance between himself and those ideas. The result was a new emphasis on "measure," which suddenly had to do double duty as a term for prosodic "minutiae" and as a conceptual basket for Williams's meditations on other aspects of the will toward order. The theory and mythology of measure, then, took shape in response to, among others, Pound. Pound is not the only poet Williams answers with measure, but more than other contemporaries Pound stood in Williams's mind for the crossing of poetic theory with social and political thought, a crossing that the theory of measure acknowledges but reexamines. Many of Williams's statements about measure have social and political implications, some of which he overstates for dramatic effect, but those implications do not eclipse his aesthetic concerns. This difference between Williams and Pound is the hidden subject of the "Without invention" passage in *Paterson*, the rhetorical structure of which suggests a reply to Pound's Canto 45:

> With usura hath no man a house of good stone
> each block cut smooth and well fitting
> that design might cover their face,
> with usura
> hath no man a painted paradise on his church wall
> *harpes et luz* . . .
> with usura the line grows thick
> with usura is no clear demarcation
> and no man can find site for his dwelling.
> Stonecutter is kept from his stone
> weaver is kept from his loom . . .
>
> Usura slayeth the child in the womb
> It stayeth the young man's courting
> It hath brought palsey to bed, lyeth
> between the young bride and her bridegroom.
>   CONTRA NATURAM

Although Pound may appear to be adopting the manner of a medieval or renaissance preacher here, anaphora, parallelism, and cataloguing once again suggest the influence of Whitman, to whom Pound had reconciled himself in "A Pact" (1913), requesting, "Let there be commerce between us." As the "commerce" between Pound and Whitman—the economic metaphor is telling—appears in the rhetorical schemes of Canto 45, so does the commerce between Williams and Pound appear in the rhetorical schemes of "Without invention." The similarities in surface patterning, however, only intensify the differences in thought, differences that begin with Williams's substitution of the antithetical construction "Without invention" for Pound's "With usura." Whereas Pound concentrates on the negative implications of an economic presence, Williams addresses the negative implications of an aesthetic absence. Pound's poem places men and women in the midst of economic, social, and historical forces. Williams's answer replaces images of men and women with images of stars, witch-hazel, alder, and mice, and it replaces economic, social, and historical forces with psychological and expressive ones. Pound's rhetoric realizes itself through tropes of production, Williams's through tropes of perception. These contrasts reflect the larger difference between Pound's conception of order and Williams's conception of measure, a difference also reflected here by the two treatments of "the line." When Pound declares "with usura the line grows thick," it is not obvious that he means the verse line, if indeed he does. Instead, the line grown thick serves as an image of the breakdown of "clear demarcation" between what is natural and what is, in Pound's view, a sin against nature. On the other hand, by the time Williams urges that "without invention the line / will never again take on its ancient / divisions," it is clear that he means the verse line and, with it, the minutiae of formal scheme. This is not to say that Williams no longer shares Pound's concern with economic and social orders; *Paterson* demonstrates repeatedly that he does. Rather, the differences between these two passages suggest that, for Williams, the path toward order, the ultimate order of "the word, a supple word," leads through the formal surface of his art.

If in Williams's mind Pound stood for the crossing of poetic theory with social and political thought, then Eliot stood for the limits and restraints of tradition. The theory of measure is as much an answer to Eliot as it is to Pound, but with this difference: while it widened the gap between Pound and Williams, despite an early closeness, the expansion of the term "measure" closed the gap between Eliot and Williams, despite a professed distance. Williams's unilateral campaign against *The Waste Land* and its author often discourages or distracts us from making important connections between the two poets; yet the vehemence of Williams's attack amounts to too much protesting, as though he found himself, much to his discomfort and annoyance, closely connected with Eliot in several ways. The point is not to assign either poet the role of originator and the other of imitator, but rather to identify features of Williams's theory of measure that seem to answer Eliot. Despite his immense learning and magisterial indifference to Williams, Eliot, too, has his limitations as a theoretician. Neither Eliot nor any of his critics has defined or adequately explained, for example, the difference between emotion and feeling ("Tradition and the Individual Talent"), an objective correlative ("Hamlet and His Problems"), or all the meanings of "music" ("The Music of Poetry"). Each of these terms poses interpretive problems, just as Williams's use of measure does. For this discussion, however, we need only remember that each poet interested himself deeply in the problems of modern verse schemes; that each poet was aware of the other; and that the two poets shared more than either cared to admit.

About the time Williams composed "Let Us Order Our World," Eliot delivered and published his lecture "The Music of Poetry" (1942). Mariani asserts that when Williams read it, he became convinced that Eliot was stealing from him. Whatever the merit of Williams's belief, he encountered "The Music of Poetry" at the crucial period when measure was expanding from term to theory. Many of the formulations he found in Eliot's lecture, whether they were indeed his or merely reflected his thinking, must have accelerated Williams's progress toward a theoretical platform of his own. Several times, for example, Eliot acknowledges "the law that poetry must not stray too far from the everyday language which we use and hear"; he echoes one of Williams's favorite formulations in speaking of the task of exploring "the relation of the idiom of verse to that of speech." When Eliot asserts, "The music of poetry, then, must be a music latent in the common speech of its time," he gives "music" a figurative meaning which Williams enlarges in "The Desert Music." When Eliot argues that "no poet can write a poem of amplitude unless he is a master of the prosaic," he gestures back to *The Waste Land* and confirms Williams's own discoveries. When Eliot traces the development of Shakespeare's style "from artificiality to simplicity, from stiffness to suppleness," he endorses the same quality Williams values in a supple word. But finally, and most important, when Eliot claims that "no verse is free for the man who wants to do a good job," he touches one of Williams's nerves.

In "The Music of Poetry" Eliot notes that he had expressed his view on free verse twenty-five years earlier, an allusion to "Reflections on *Vers Libre*," published in 1917, the same year as Williams's essay "America, Whitman, and the Art of Poetry." In 1917 both poets agreed that good verse is never wholly free, but their subsequent arguments differ. Eliot's conclusion is that "There is no escape from metre; there is only mastery." He arrives at this conclusion, having made these assertions:

> But the most interesting verse which has yet been written in our language has been done either by taking a very simple form, like the iambic pentameter, and constantly withdrawing from it, or taking no form at all, and constantly approximating to a very simple one. It is this contrast between fixity and flux, this unperceived evasion of monotony, which is the very life of verse. . . .

> We may therefore formulate as follows: the ghost of some simple
> metre should lurk behind the arras in even the "freest" verse; to ad-
> vance menacingly as we doze, and withdraw as we rouse. Or, free-
> dom is only truly freedom when it appears against the background
> of an artificial limitation.

In 1917 Williams could not offer a theoretical alternative either to free verse or
Eliot's arguments. Instead, his reply to Eliot unfolds during the next forty years
in his theory of measure. In Eliot's terse formulations, Williams found himself
confronted with two propositions, one of which he wanted to reject and the
other to absorb. "Reflections on *Vers Libre*" pressured him to shape a response
not only to Eliot but also to the tradition for which, in Williams's mind, Eliot
stood.

The proposition which Williams could never bring himself to accept is that
there is no escape from meter. Eliot's metrical ghost lurking behind the arras is,
Williams argues, the phantom we can afford to be haunted by no longer, particularly the ghost of iambic pentameter: "We do not live in a sonnet world; we
do not live even in an iambic world; certainly not a world of iambic pentameters."
While this statement assumes a questionable relation between the historical world
and poetic convention, it also carries with it another meaning. For Williams
iambic pentameter amounts to much more than an old-fashioned verse scheme
which does not easily accommodate the American idiom; it also stands for the
entire tradition of English poetry from Chaucer to Tennyson. More than that,
Williams associates iambic pentameter with the twentieth-century representative
of that tradition, T. S. Eliot. His repeated denials of the pentameter, echoing
Pound, mask his anti-Eliot polemic. In turn, this polemic is one of the major
pressures shaping the theory of measure. The fiction of a "variable foot" allows
Williams to have it both ways, as he appears to escape from meter and Eliot,
while maintaining the necessary "contrast between fixity and flux," which Eliot
—or before him Poe in "The Rationale of Verse"—considers the very life of
verse. Williams's theory of measure then is, as well as an answer to Whitman and
Pound, a theoretical apparatus designed to support a public response to Eliot.

The world is not iambic, the psyche is not iambic, the heartbeat is not
iambic, breathing is not iambic, but the tradition is iambic. There is no escape
from this truth, and Williams knew it, even in 1917 when in "America, Whitman, and the Art of Poetry" he seems to speak directly to Eliot: "But if by 'too
much freedom' they mean that a man binds himself by ignoring truths he cannot
escape, no matter how hard he may run, then I will listen." Williams did listen,
and he heard, too. One of the great ironies of his career is that more than many
of his contemporaries and self-proclaimed heirs Williams mastered meter, which,

according to Eliot in "Reflections on *Vers Libre*," means mastering the "constant evasion and recognition of regularity." Enjambment, asymmetric typography, excursions into prose, the use of the vernacular, his own theoretical statements— all these are strategies to evade an iambic norm; and yet time and time again, as in "Seafarer," "The Wind Increases," "Good Night," *Paterson*, "The Desert Music," and *Asphodel*, he recognizes that norm, allowing it "to advance menacingly as we doze, and withdraw as we rouse." When one thinks of modern masters of the iambic meter, one thinks of Yeats, Eliot, Frost, Stevens, and Crane. But the very fact that Williams does not appear on such a list—that he would not want to—confirms the success of his evasion. Unlike these others, Williams grounds himself not in metricality but in nonmetricality. Against this background moments of iambic regularity become significant variations. As with many successful evasions, however, the most important act of concealment involves truth we conceal from ourselves. This is another crucial aspect of the theory of measure: the higher Williams piled letters, notes, essays, and poems preaching the escape from meter, the deeper he buried the truth in his own mind.

If Eliot's proposition that there is no escape from meter is one Williams wanted to deny, then this is the proposition he wanted to absorb and master: "Or, freedom is only truly freedom when it appears against the background of an artificial limitation." The theory of measure is predicated on this belief; Williams's fifty-year search for measure is a search for limitation, the ground against which his figures of freedom can appear. In "Let Us Order Our World" he claims to seek "limitless expansion" and release from restraints which destroy; yet in his essay, "Free Verse" (significantly, he lists "Reflections on *Vers Libre*" in the short bibliography following the essay), he locates the origin of measure in the war between freedom and discipline. This opposition would seem to point toward Eliot's "Reflections on *Vers Libre*"; yet beyond Eliot stands the American prophet of limitation, Emerson.

In various ways Poe, Whitman, Pound, and Eliot all contributed, either directly or indirectly, to the multiple meanings of measure. Williams acknowledges each of these poets, mentions them frequently, and holds their images before him as he assembles his thoughts on the nature of verse. But Williams mentions Emerson rarely. In the *Selected Letters*, for example, his name appears once in a letter to Thirlwall (June 13, 1955), and even then he is mentioned only in passing:

> The history of American prosody shows itself to have been troubled by a concern for something wrong with our acceptance of verse forms handed down to us. Emerson was another in that sequence. Poe was another American poet who was made uneasy by the structure of verses and wrote an essay about its mathematical implications. Most

were content to imitate their betters, the asses, and as a consequence
wrote slavishly.

Throughout his writings Williams remains strangely quiet about Emerson, who
does not seem to be either a major contributor to the theory of measure or someone Williams seeks to challenge with that theory. He is merely "another in that
sequence." Presumably, Emerson's statement in "The Poet" that "it is not meters,
but a meter-making argument that makes a poem" would be welcome as another
formulation in favor of a new measure, but Williams does not pounce on this
passage and subject it to any sustained examination. One might be tempted,
therefore, to grant Emerson a certain minimal importance as an earlier American
poet, and then to dismiss him. Mariani, for example, discusses Williams's affilia-
tion with the Unitarian church and the tradition that shaped Emerson. Later, he
also alludes to Williams's "Emersonian bias"; yet, except for a few other isolated
references, this is all we hear. The problem, however, is that while Emerson
himself may seem to have little to do with Williams's theory of measure, Emersonianism has everything to do with it. At the core of Williams's search for measure
lies the American pragmatic effort to reconcile freedom with limitation.

In tracing the shadow of Emersonianism, we might recall a passage from
Spring and All: "The inevitable flux of the seeing eye toward measuring itself by
the world it inhabits can only result in himself crushing humiliation unless the
individual raise to some approximate co-extension with the universe. This is possible by aid of the imagination." Emerson's name does not appear in *Spring and
All*, but Emersonianism stamps this passage. In the arrangement of the seeing eye,
the individual, the world or universe, and the imagination, emerges a distinctly
Emersonian configuration. Through the agency of the seeing eye, or visionary
faculty, the individual self realizes the antithetical relation which exists between
itself and the world or universe (Emerson's Nature, or Not Me). This realization
begets in the self a drive to defend itself against the power of the universe to
crush and humiliate it. According to Williams, this defense "is possible by the aid
of the imagination." Whereas Emerson might have said "Reason" instead of
"imagination," he makes the link between them clear in "Nature": "The Imagination may be defined to be the use which the Reason makes of the material
world." In the Emersonian economy of *Spring and All*, measurements "can only
result in" a confrontation between the freedom of the individual and limitations
the universe imposes on that freedom. The challenge to the individual, then, is
to rise "to some approximate co-extension with the universe," or, as Emerson
would say, to discover power in self-reliance.

The Emersonian quality of Williams's thinking here is not limited to an
apparent coincidence of attitudes; it also registers a striking rhetorical resonance.

In 1866, for example, Emerson notes in his journal: "But I am always struck with the fact that mind delights in measuring itself thus with matter,—with history. A thought, any thought, pressed, followed, opened, dwarfs nature, custom, and all but itself." As in the passage from *Spring and All*, measurement does not merely imply comparison with a standard; rather, it signifies a competitive struggle between the mind and matter, the former measuring itself and its freedom against the latter. This competitive, combative meaning of measure also surfaces in the essay "Fate," Emerson's most sustained meditation on freedom and its limits:

> History is the action and reaction of these two,—Nature and Thought; two boys pushing each other on the curbstone of the pavement. Everything is pusher or pushed; and matter and mind are in perpetual tilt and balance, so. Whilst the man is weak, the earth takes up him. He plants his brain and affections. By and by he will take up the earth, and have his gardens and vineyards in the beautiful order and productiveness of his thought. Every solid in the universe is ready to become fluid on the approach of the mind, and the power to flux it is the measure of the mind.

Emerson's assertion that the power "to flux" matter is the measure of the mind prefigures Williams's notion of the "inevitable flux" of the seeing eye toward measuring itself by the world. In the Emersonian arena, the freedom of flux, or fluidity, contends with the limitation of solidity. There is no easy coexistence possible between them, only constant struggle. When the mind measures itself against matter, it necessarily enters that struggle.

This Emersonian meaning of measure also informs Williams's theory of verse schemes, as well it might, because the life of verse depends on the contrast between fixity and flux. When Williams describes freedom and discipline, his name for limitation, as "warring elements," he states what is at stake for him in a poem. As the patterns of verse combine fixity and flux, limitation and freedom, they dramatize the larger Emersonian contest between mind and matter, or between the imagination and the world. As verse measurement assigns dominant power to fixity or flux in a particular poem, by grounding it in metricality or nonmetricality, it becomes, as Emerson would say, a measure of the mind. Now, if this is so, we might wonder why Williams would insist that there be discipline, fixity, or limitation in verse, when he is so outspoken a champion of freedom. Wouldn't it be more fitting to dispense with these altogether? The simplest answer to this is Eliot's: freedom cannot be recognized unless it appears against a background of artificial limitation. The regulation between freedom and limitation, he implies, is binary. Thus, for example, we might argue that without at least the implication of a fixed norm, a variation cannot appear as a gesture of freedom. Without an assumed norm, the argument would go, the poem presents nothing but confusion and apparent randomness, which is not the same as freedom. But, although this argument has a certain obvious truth to it, it fails to explain Williams's particular attitude toward limitation, an attitude that is essentially Emersonian.

In "Fate" Emerson is not concerned with artificial limitations; he is preoccupied with real ones:

> We cannot trifle with this reality, this cropping-out in our planted gardens of the core of the world. No picture of life can have any veracity that does not admit the odious facts. A man's power is hooped in by a necessity which, by many experiments, he touches on every side until he learns its arc.
>
> The element running through entire nature, which we popularly call Fate, is known to us as limitation. Whatever limits us we call Fate.

Several years after "Self-Reliance," his rhapsodic hymn to freedom, Emerson finds himself admitting the odious facts of fate. These he traces "in matter, mind, and morals; in race, in retardations of strata, and in thought and character as well." The point of Emerson's argument, however, is to convince us that "limitation is power," that quickly "fate slides into freedom and freedom into fate," and that it is "the best use of Fate to teach a fatal courage." Finally, with an interesting choice of words, Emerson returns to the relation between limits and measurements: "We can afford to allow the limitation, if we know it is the meter of the growing man. We stand against Fate, as children stand up against the wall in their father's house and notch their height from year to year. But when the boy grows to man, and is master of the house, he pulls down that wall and builds a new and bigger. 'Tis only a question of time." Here Emerson's word for measurement is "meter," the term that shuttles between the world of measurements and numbers and the world of verse. As meter is limitation in verse, limitation is meter in life. We can afford to allow this meter in the poems of our lives, as long as we realize that it measures our growth and does not suppress it.

For Williams measure carries, in addition to its other meanings, the connotations of Emersonian fate, the meter of our lives by which we know we have grown. When Williams concedes that a man may bind himself by ignoring truths he cannot escape, he acknowledges the presence of limitations, real not artificial. Several years after "America, Whitman, and the Art of Poetry," the older Williams, like the older Emerson, has to admit the odious fact of real limitations. The enlargement of measure into a private philosophy accompanies this admission. The theory of measure, with its many overlapping layers and twisting ramifications, represents Williams's attempt to teach himself a fatal courage, a courage that pervades, for example, "The Ivy Crown": "We are only mortal / but being mortal / can defy our fate." Limitation is power, in verse and in life, and measure is limitation. When Williams declares that without measure we are lost, he erases distinctions between the artificial limitations of prosodic convention and the real limitations of human existence. To measure is all Williams knows, and, in saying so at the end of *Paterson*, he answers Keats, the poet he first admired: not beauty or truth, but measure. Measure is all we know on earth, and all we need to know.

The last poem in which the word "measure" appears offers a parable about freedom, limitation, and poetry:

Heel & Toe to the End

Gagarin says, in ecstasy,
he could have
gone on forever

he floated
ate and sang
and when he emerged from that

one hundred eight minutes off
the surface of
the earth he was smiling

Then he returned
to take his place
among the rest of us

from all that division and
subtraction a measure
toe and heel

heel and toe he felt
as if he had
been dancing

Published in July of 1961, "Heel & Toe to the End" celebrates the flight of Yuri Alekseyevitch Gagarin, Soviet cosmonaut and first man to orbit the earth in space. Once again, Williams finds in the advances of science and technology a metaphor for poetry and the poet. Gagarin also represents the explorer-discoverer, the hero of Williams's imagination and a twentieth-century version of Columbus. Here, however, exploration and discovery have not yielded the new world of North

America, but a new world of space, the Einsteinian realm where all measurements are relative. In addition to these familiar figurations, Williams uses familiar schemes: nonmetrical verse ruled by enjambment, by variations in line lengths, and by the tripartite format of three-line stanzas; and yet, against the background of nonmetricality shimmers the iambic mirage:

> Then he returned
>
> to táke his pláce
>
> amóng the rest of ús

As suddenly as it appears, the metrical phantom dissolves into a meditation on measure, but its significance remains. "Heel & Toe to the End" falls into two halves: the first describes Gagarin's flight and ecstasy; the second, marked by the capitalized "Then," considers his return to "his place among the rest of us." After the ecstatic voyage up and out, during which the lone self floats, sings, and wants to go on forever, comes the return to the place of the self among other selves. The verse becomes iambic as the freedom of Gagarin's discovery slides back into the fate of his ordinary life. But nothing in the poem suggests that the descent into limitation represents defeat. Instead, the poem moves from limitation to measure. As in *Paterson* or "The Desert Music," measure returns us to counting ("all that division and / subtraction") and to the foot, the ancient division of dance. In his ecstasy the explorer felt "as if he had / been dancing," as if his excitement found release, not restraint, in the regularity of aesthetic organization. The chiasmus "toe and heel // heel and toe" not only mimes the dance of the weightless cosmonaut; it also traces the chiastic pattern of restraint sliding into release, release into restraint. In his search for measure Williams traced this pattern many times; he watched it dance through his poems, heel and toe, to the end, as he sought to fashion out of the warring elements of freedom and discipline a principle to organize his poems and his experience. That a poem, like a life, must pattern itself in new ways when older ones fail is the discovery he made in his explorations of himself and his world. It is a discovery he brought back each time he returned to take his place among the rest of us.

Chronology

1883	William Carlos Williams is born September 17 in Rutherford, New Jersey to William George Williams, born in England and brought up in the West Indies, and Raquel Hélène Hoheb Williams, born in Puerto Rico.
1897–99	Attends schools in Switzerland and Paris.
1902	Graduates from Horace Mann High School in New York City.
1902–6	Studies at the Medical School of the University of Pennsylvania. While completing his M.D., he becomes acquainted with Ezra Pound, Hilda Doolittle, and Charles Demuth. Works on imitation of Keats's *Endymion*.
1906–9	Interns at the old French Hospital and at the Nursery and Child's Hospital in New York City.
1909	His first volume, *Poems*, printed privately. Goes to Europe to study pediatrics in Leipzig and to visit his brother in Rome and Ezra Pound in London.
1910	Begins his medical practice in Rutherford.
1912	Marries Florence Herman.
1913	*The Tempers* is published in England. Williams contributes poems to numerous little magazines during the following decade.
1914	Pound's *Des Imagistes* anthology includes "Postlude." "The Wanderer" is published in *The Egoist*.
1917	*Al Que Quiere! A Book of Poems* is published.
1920	*Kora in Hell: Improvisations* is published. Williams edits *Contact* with Robert McAlmon (until 1923).

161

1921   *Sour Grapes* is published.

1922   T. S. Eliot's *The Waste Land* is published.

1923   *Spring and All*, *The Great American Novel*, and *Go Go* are published.

1924   Williams makes a third trip to Europe with his wife. He meets James Joyce, Ernest Hemingway, George Antheil, Ford Madox Ford, Philippe Soupault, Gertrude Stein, and others.

1925   *In the American Grain* is published. Williams joins the staff of the Passaic General Hospital while maintaining his general practice.

1926   Receives the Dial Award. *Dial* publishes "Paterson," a precursor of the later poem.

1928   *A Voyage to Pagany* is published.

1929   Philippe Soupault's *Last Nights of Paris*, translated from the French by Williams, is published.

1931   Williams receives the Guarantor's Prize from *Poetry*.

1932   *The Cod Head; A Novelette and Other Prose*; and *The Knife of the Times* are published. Williams, McAlmon, and Nathanael West edit the revival of *Contact*.

1934   *Collected Poems 1921–1931* is published with a preface by Wallace Stevens.

1935   *An Early Martyr* is published.

1936   *Adam & Eve & The City* and *The First President*, a libretto, are published.

1937   *White Mule* is published.

1938   *Life along the Passaic River* and *The Complete Collected Poems* are published.

1940–45 *In the Money*, *The Broken Span*, *Trial Horse No. 1* (later titled *Many Loves*), and *The Wedge* are published during these years.

1946   *Paterson, Book One* is published.

1948   *A Dream of Love*; *Paterson, Book Two*; and "The Clouds" are published. Williams suffers a heart attack. Pound's *Pisan Cantos* are published.

1949   Williams is made a Fellow of the Library of Congress. *The Pink Church*; *Paterson, Book Three*; and *Selected Poems* are published.

1950   Williams receives the first National Book Award for Poetry (for *Paterson, Book Three* and *Selected Poems*). *Make Light of It* and *Collected Later Poems* are published.

1951   *The Collected Earlier Poems*; *Paterson, Book Four*; and *Autobiography* are published. A series of strokes forces Williams to abandon his medical practice to his son Bill, Jr.

1952   Appointed Consultant in Poetry to the Library of Congress. *The Build-Up* is published.

1953   Williams receives the Bollingen Award for Poetry.

1954   *The Desert Music* and *Selected Essays* are published. Williams also publishes a translation, in collaboration with his mother, of Don Francisco de Quevedo's *A Dog and the Fever*.

1955   Williams makes a reading tour of colleges across the country. *Journey to Love* is published.

1957–58   *The Selected Letters*; *Paterson, Book Five*; and *I Wanted to Write a Poem* are published during these years.

1959   *Many Loves* runs in repertory at the Living Theatre in New York. *Yes, Mrs. Williams* is published.

1961–62   *The Farmers' Daughters*, *Many Loves and Other Plays*, and *Pictures from Brueghel* are published.

1963   Williams dies on March 4 in Rutherford, New Jersey. Awarded the Pulitzer Prize for *Pictures from Brueghel*, posthumously. *Paterson* is published, including the notes for Book Six.

Contributors

HAROLD BLOOM, Sterling Professor of the Humanities at Yale University, is the author of *The Anxiety of Influence*, *Poetry and Repression*, and many other volumes of literary criticism. His forthcoming study, *Freud: Transference and Authority*, attempts a full-scale reading of all of Freud's major writings. A MacArthur Prize Fellow, he is general editor of five series of literary criticism published by Chelsea House.

LOUIS L. MARTZ is Sterling Professor of English Emeritus at Yale University. His numerous books include *The Poetry of Meditation*, *The Paradise Within*, and *The Poem of the Mind*.

J. HILLIS MILLER is Frederick W. Hilles Professor of English and Comparative Literature at Yale University. His books of criticism include *Poets of Reality: Six Twentieth-Century Writers*, *Fiction and Repetition*, and *The Linguistic Moment*.

THOMAS R. WHITAKER is Professor of English at Yale University and the author of *Swan and Shadow: Yeats' Dialogue with History* and *William Carlos Williams*.

JOSEPH N. RIDDEL is Professor of English at the University of California at Los Angeles and the author of *The Clairvoyant Eye: The Poetry and Poetics of Wallace Stevens* and *The Inverted Bell: Modernism and the Counterpoetics of William Carlos Williams*.

PAUL MARIANI is Professor of English at the University of Massachusetts. His work on Williams includes *William Carlos Williams: The Poet and His Critics*, the biography *William Carlos Williams: A New World Naked*, and *A Usable Past: Essays on Modern and Contemporary Poetry*.

DONALD HALL is a poet and essayist and the editor of numerous poetry anthologies. His books of criticism include *Goatfoot, Milktongue, Twinbird*, and *The Weather for Poetry*.

JOHN W. ERWIN is the author of *Lyric Apocalypse: Reconstruction in Ancient and Modern Poetry*.

STEPHEN CUSHMAN is Assistant Professor of English at the University of Virginia. He is the author of *William Carlos Williams and the Meanings of Measure*.

Bibliography

Angoff, Charles, ed. *William Carlos Williams: Papers by Kenneth Burke, Emily Mitchell Wallace, Norman Holmes Pearson, A. M. Sullivan.* Madison, N. J.: Fairleigh Dickinson University Press, 1974.

Bollier, E. P. "Against the American Grain: William Carlos Williams between Whitman and Poe." *Tulane Studies in English* 23 (1978): 123–42.

Bové, Paul. "The World and Earth of William Carlos Williams: *Paterson* as a 'Long Poem.'" *Genre* 11 (1978): 575–96.

Breslin, James E. *William Carlos Williams: An American Artist.* New York: Oxford University Press, 1970.

Brinnin, John Malcolm. *William Carlos Williams.* Minneapolis: University of Minnesota Press, 1963.

Bruns, Gerald L. "De Improvisatione." *The Iowa Review* 9, no. 3 (1978): 66–78.

Burke, Kenneth. "William Carlos Williams: 1883–1963." *New York Review of Books* 1, no. 2 (1963): 45–47.

Cambon, Glauco. *The Inclusive Flame: Studies in American Poetry.* Bloomington: Indiana University Press, 1963.

Coffman, Stanley I. *Imagism: A Chapter for the History of Modern Poetry.* Norman: University of Oklahoma Press, 1951.

Coles, Robert. *William Carlos Williams: The Knack of Survival in America.* New Brunswick, N. J.: Rutgers University Press, 1975.

Conarroe, Joel. *William Carlos Williams' "Paterson": Language and Landscape.* Philadelphia: University of Pennsylvania Press, 1970.

Creeley, Robert. "The Fact of His Life." *The Nation* 195 (October 13, 1962): 224.

Cushman, Stephen. *William Carlos Williams and the Meanings of Measure.* New Haven: Yale University Press, 1985.

Dembo, L. S. "William Carlos Williams: Objectivist Mathematics." In *Conceptions of Reality in Modern American Poetry.* Berkeley: University of California Press, 1966.

Dijkstra, Bram. *The Hieroglyphics of a New Speech: Cubism, Stieglitz, and the Early Poetry of William Carlos Williams.* Princeton: Princeton University Press, 1969.

Donahue, Denis. *Connoisseurs of Chaos: Ideas of Order in Modern American Poetry.* New York: Macmillan, 1965.

Doyle, Charles. *William Carlos Williams: The Critical Heritage.* London: Routledge & Kegan Paul, 1980.

Engels, John, ed. *Studies in "Paterson."* Columbus, Ohio: Charles E. Merrill, 1971. *Field* 29 (Fall 1983).

Friedman, Melvin J., and John B. Vickery, eds. *The Shaken Realist: Essays in Modern Literature in Honor of Frederick J. Hoffman.* Baton Rouge: Louisiana State University Press, 1970.

Guimond, James. *The Art of William Carlos Williams: A Discovery and Possession of America.* Urbana: University of Illinois Press, 1968.

Hollander, John. "The Poem in the Eye." *Shenandoah* 23, no. 3 (1972): 3–32.

Jarrell, Randall. *Poetry and the Age.* New York: Vintage, 1955.

Jauss, David. "The Descent, the Dance, and the Wheel: The Aesthetic Theory of William Carlos Williams' *Kora in Hell.*" *Boston University Journal* 25, no. 1 (1977): 37–42.

Joswick, Thomas P. "Beginning with Loss: The Poetics of William Carlos Williams' *Kora in Hell: Improvisations.*" *Texas Studies in Literature and Language* 19, no. 1 (1977): 98–118.

Juhasz, Suzanne. *Metaphor and the Poetry of Williams, Pound, and Stevens.* Lewisburg, Penn.: Bucknell University Press, 1974.

Kenner, Hugh. *Gnomon.* New York: McDowell, Obolensky, 1958.

———. *A Homemade World: The American Modernist Writers.* New York: Alfred A. Knopf, 1975.

Koch, Vivienne. *William Carlos Williams.* Norfolk, Conn.: New Directions, 1950.

Kronick, Joseph G. "William Carlos Williams' Search for an 'American' Place." In *American Poetics of History: From Emerson to the Moderns.* Baton Rouge: Louisiana State University Press, 1984.

Levertov, Denise. "William Carlos Williams 1883–1963" and "William Carlos Williams and the Duende." In *The Poet and the World.* New York: New Directions, 1973.

Levin, Harry. "William Carlos Williams and the Old World." In *Memories of the Moderns.* New York: New Directions, 1980.

The Literary Review 1, no. 1 (Autumn 1957).

Lowell, Robert. "William Carlos Williams." *The Hudson Review* 14 (Winter 1961–62): 530–36.

Mariani, Paul L. *William Carlos Williams: A New World Naked.* New York: McGraw-Hill, 1981.

———. *William Carlos Williams: The Poet and His Critics.* Chicago: American Library Association, 1975.

Marling, William. *William Carlos Williams and the Painters, 1909–1923.* Athens, Ohio: Ohio University Press, 1982.

Martz, Louis L. *The Poem of the Mind.* New York: Oxford University Press, 1966.

Massachusetts Review 3, no. 2 (Winter 1962).

Mazzaro, Jerome, ed. *Profile of William Carlos Williams.* Columbus, Ohio: Charles E. Merrill, 1971.

———. *William Carlos Williams: The Later Poems.* Ithaca, N. Y.: Cornell University Press, 1973.

Miller, J. Hillis. *Poets of Reality.* Cambridge: The Belknap Press of Harvard University, 1966.

———. *William Carlos Williams: A Collection of Critical Essays.* Englewood Cliffs, N. J.: Prentice-Hall, 1966.

————. "Williams." In *The Linguistic Moment*. Princeton: Princeton University Press, 1985.

Morgan, Richard J. "Chaos and Order: The Cycle of Life and Art in Williams' *Spring and All*." *Interpretations* 11 (1979): 35–51.

Ostrom, Alan. *The Poetic World of William Carlos Williams*. Carbondale: Southern Illinois University Press, 1966.

Paul, Sherman. *The Music of Survival: A Biography of a Poem by William Carlos Williams*. Urbana: University of Illinois Press, 1968.

Pearce, Roy Harvey. *The Continuity of American Poetry*. Princeton: Princeton University Press, 1961.

Peterson, Walter S. *An Approach to* Paterson. New Haven: Yale University Press, 1967.

Pound, Ezra. "Dr. Williams' Position." In *Literary Essays*, edited by T. S. Eliot. Norfolk, Conn.: New Directions, 1954.

Pratt, William, ed. *The Imagist Poem*. New York: E. P. Dutton, 1963.

Quinn, Sister Mary Bernetta. *The Metamorphic Tradition in Modern Poetry*. New Brunswick, N. J.: Rutgers University Press, 1955.

Rapp, Carl. *William Carlos Williams and Romantic Idealism*. Hanover, N. H.: University Press of New England, 1984.

Rexroth, Kenneth. *Assays*. Norfolk, Conn.: New Directions, 1961.

Riddel, Joseph N. *The Inverted Bell: Modernism and the Counterpoetics of William Carlos Williams*. Baton Rouge: Louisiana State University Press, 1974.

————. " 'Keep Your Pecker Up'—*Paterson Five* and the Question of Metapoetry." *Glyph* 8 (1981): 203–31.

Sankey, Benjamin. *A Companion to William Carlos Williams'* Paterson. Berkeley: University of California Press, 1971.

Sayre, Henry M. "Ready-Mades and Other Measures: The Poetics of Marcel Duchamp and William Carlos Williams." *Journal of Modern Literature* 8, no. 1 (1980): 3–22.

Shapiro, Karl. "The True Contemporary." In *Start with the Sun*. Lincoln: University of Nebraska Press, 1963.

Simpson, Louis. *Three on the Tower: The Lives and Works of Ezra Pound, T. S. Eliot, and William Carlos Williams*. New York: William Morrow, 1975.

Slate, Joseph Evans. "William Carlos Williams, Hart Crane, and the Virtue of History." *Texas Studies in Literature and Language* 6 (1965): 486–511.

Sutton, Walter. "Dr. Williams' *Paterson* and the Quest for Form." *Criticism* 2 (Summer 1960): 242–59.

Tomlinson, Charles, ed. *William Carlos Williams: A Critical Anthology*. Harmondsworth: Penguin Books, 1972.

Townley, Rod. *The Early Poetry of William Carlos Williams*. Ithaca, N. Y.: Cornell University Press, 1975.

Waggoner, Hyatt H. "William Carlos Williams: Naturalizing the Unearthly." In *American Visionary Poetry*. Baton Rouge: Louisiana State University Press, 1982.

Wagner, Linda Welshimer. *The Poems of William Carlos Williams: A Critical Study*. Middletown, Conn.: Wesleyan University Press, 1964.

————. *The Prose of William Carlos Williams*. Middletown, Conn.: Wesleyan University Press, 1970.

————. *William Carlos Williams: A Reference Guide*. Boston: G. K. Hall, 1978.

Wallace, Emily Mitchell. *A Bibliography of William Carlos Williams.* Middletown, Conn.: Wesleyan University Press, 1968.

Weatherhead, A. Kingsley. *The Edge of the Image: Marianne Moore, William Carlos Williams, and Some Other Poets.* Seattle: University of Washington Press, 1967.

Weaver, Mike. *William Carlos Williams: The American Background.* London: Cambridge University Press, 1971.

Whitaker, Thomas R. *William Carlos Williams.* New York: Twayne Publishing Co., 1968.

Whittemore, Reed. *William Carlos Williams, Poet from Jersey.* Boston: Houghton Mifflin, 1975.

Willard, Nancy. *Testimony of the Invisible Man: William Carlos Williams, Francis Ponge, Rainer Maria Rilke, Pablo Neruda.* Columbia: University of Missouri Press, 1970.

The William Carlos Williams Review (formerly *Newsletter*), 1975–.

Acknowledgments

"The Unicorn in *Paterson*" (originally entitled "The Unicorn in *Paterson*: William Carlos Williams") by Louis L. Martz from *Thought* 35, no. 139 (Winter 1960), © 1960 by Fordham University Press. Reprinted by permission of the publisher.

"Williams: Poet of Reality" (originally entitled "William Carlos Williams") by J. Hillis Miller from *Poets of Reality* by J. Hillis Miller, © 1965 by the President and Fellows of Harvard College. Reprinted by permission of The Belknap Press of Harvard University Press. "The Yellow Chimney" by William Carlos Williams from *Collected Later Poems: 1914–1950*, © 1944 by William Carlos Williams. "The Locust Tree in Flower" by William Carlos Williams from *Collected Earlier Poems: Before 1914*, © 1938 by New Directions Publishing Corporation. Both poems are reprinted by permission of New Directions Publishing Corporation.

"New Worlds" by Thomas R. Whitaker from *William Carlos Williams* by Thomas R. Whitaker, © 1968 by Twayne Publishers, Inc. Reprinted by permission of Twayne Publishers, a division of G. K. Hall & Co., Boston.

"Williams and the Ek-stasy of Beginnings" (originally entitled "The Ek-stasy of Beginnings") by Joseph N. Riddel from *The Inverted Bell: Modernism and the Counter-poetics of William Carlos Williams* by Joseph N. Riddel, © 1974 by Louisiana State University Press. Reprinted by permission.

"The Eighth Day of Creation: Rethinking *Paterson*" by Paul Mariani from *Twentieth Century Literature* 21, no. 3 (1975), © 1975 by Hofstra University Press. Reprinted by permission. This essay later appeared in *A Usable Past: Essays on Modern and Contemporary Poetry* (University of Massachusetts Press, 1984).

"William Carlos Williams and the Visual" by Donald Hall from *Field* 29 (Fall 1983), © 1983 by Oberlin College. Reprinted by permission. "Nantucket" by William Carlos Williams from *Collected Earlier Poems: Before 1914*, © 1938 by New Directions Publishing Corporation. Reprinted by permission of New Directions Publishing Corporation.

"William Carlos Williams and Europe" by John W. Erwin from *Lyric Apocalypse: Reconstruction in Ancient and Modern Poetry* by John W. Erwin, © 1984 by Scholars Press. Reprinted by permission.

"The World Is Not Iambic: Measure as Trope" (originally entitled "The World Is Not Iambic") by Stephen Cushman from *William Carlos Williams and the Meaning of Measure* by Stephen Cushman, © 1985 by Yale University. Reprinted by permission of Yale University Press. "Heel & Toe to the End" by William Carlos Williams from *Pictures from Brueghel*, © 1962 by William Carlos Williams. Reprinted by permission of New Directions Publishing Corporation.

Index

173